Praise for *You're Not Doing It Right*

"All these years, Michael Ian Black has not gotten enough
credit for what a good wr[...]ning
and good company and—h[...]And
really, really funny, of cou[...]ady
guessed at that part."

— [...] *Life*

"The comedian hilariously chronicles his own missteps and
how mistakes often lead to greatness. . . . Candidly captures
vulnerability at its most hysterical."

— *Interview Magazine*

"Funny, moving, sweet, and unfailingly honest, no matter
how bad (or uncool) it makes Black look. Comedians have
mined marriage for material since there have been comedians, but Black's deeply personal memoir succeeds by going
beyond the jokes into uncomfortable places."

— *The Onion's A.V. Club*

"Memorable and funny. . . . An amusing look at masculine
insecurity and confusion."

— *Kirkus Reviews*

"Black's most personal turn yet. . . . Though *You're Not Doing
It Right* has much comedy in it, its foremost trait is its honesty—a clear-eyed truth-telling about the hardships of marriage,
the death of his father, and the frustrations of child-rearing."

—Associated Press

"The hilarious, self-deprecating autobiography tries to answer
the lingering question of 'How did I get here?'"

— *The Village Voice*

"A humorous take on Black's path from New Jersey kid through
single Manhattan guy to suburban husband and father."

— *Publishers Weekly*

"This kind of highly relatable, quick-witted memoir can easily lapse into formula. But Black's observations have more depth than one might expect. At times, he delivers moments of great tenderness and insight."

—Boston.com

"A sardonic tome. . . . Michael Ian Black will say what most people are unwilling to admit about themselves."

—*The Brooklyn Paper*

"Filled with humor, pathos, and poetic prose—revealing Black to be both an empathetic observer of the human condition and an excellent writer."

—Expressnightout.com

"Told with brutal and hilarious honesty."

—Examiner.com

"Michael Ian Black has always displayed a uniquely skewed sense of humor. Now he wants you to know the real him. Sort of."

—*Nerdist News*

"Surprisingly personal."   —*Toro Magazine*

"Here's the truth: I'm 34, been married for six years and have two sons, ages 3 and 6 months (or so), and I'm losing my fucking mind. So, what to do: Talk about my feelings to friends? Talk to my wife? Start seeing a therapist? Start drinking heavily? No, to all of the above. I'll tell you what you want to do. You ask Michael Ian Fucking Black for advice."

—*Laughspin*

"This book is so frank, so full of amusingly embarrassing confessions, I should probably be giving Michael Black a hug instead of a blurb."

—Sarah Vowell, *New York Times* bestselling author and essayist

"It's no surprise that Michael Ian Black's book is hysterical. But I was surprised by how heartfelt and touching his memoir is. It's true: Michael Ian Black has emotions!"

—A.J. Jacobs, *New York Times* bestselling author of *Drop Dead Healthy*

"I loved *My Custom Van*. But I loved *You're Not Doing It Right* even more. Reading this book felt like taking a long road trip with Michael himself—which I've done. And I actually recommend the book more. Touching, hilarious, and truthful all at once. What else do you want, America?"

—Mike Birbiglia, *New York Times* bestselling author of *Sleepwalk with Me*

"Dear Michael Ian Black: Please stop writing things in books that I wish I had written myself, it's starting to make me feel bad. Also, would you like to be friends someday? I sure would."

—Samantha Bee, senior correspondent on *The Daily Show* and author of *I Know I Am, But What Are You?*

"Michael Ian Black is one of the finest comedy minds of our generation and a master at assembling words in a hilariously pleasing way. You would have to be a vapid crapsack not to enjoy this book."

—Chris Hardwick

My Custom Van

"Michael Ian Black has proven that even the most simple-minded among us can occasionally create works of genius."

—Stephen Colbert

"Like all custom vans, Michael Ian Black's book is customized to fit your needs and wants for the journey of your life.

It's luxurious, entertaining, spooky, disturbing, and hilarious. Devil's in the details! It's stocked with tacos, vampires, squirrels, a cleaning lady, scented candles, salami, tundra, and a foreword by Abe Lincoln himself—now that's Class with a capital C. Enjoy the ride of your lifetime."

—Amy Sedaris

"Fun to read while you're pooping."

—Sarah Silverman

"Michael Ian Black is so wrong that he's right."

—Lewis Black

"Michael Ian Black takes the laughless in all of us roughly by the shoulders and INSISTS WE LAUGH, usually by writing exceedingly funny and compelling essays such as those included in this volume."

—John Hodgman

"This is a great book for shut-ins, for people who like to laugh at sentences, and people who like to move their belongings from place to place. In fact, anyone who likes to pack or ship anything will find a lot to like in these pages."

—Dave Eggers

"I always walk away jealous and a little fearful of Michael Ian Black's sharp comedic wit. If you like your comedy dry, absurd, and unforced, you will love this book."

—Jim Gaffigan

you're not doing it right

(tales of marriage, sex, death, and other humiliations)

by *new york times* bestselling author

michael ian black

gallery books

new york   london   toronto   sydney   new delhi

Gallery Books
A Division of Simon & Schuster, Inc.
1230 Avenue of the Americas
New York, NY 10020

Copyright © 2012 by Hot Schwartz Productions

First Gallery Books trade paperback edition October 2012

For information about special discounts for bulk purchases, please contact Simon & Schuster Special Sales at 1-866-506-1949 or business@simonandschuster.com.

The Simon & Schuster Speakers Bureau can bring authors to your live event. For more information or to book an event contact the Simon & Schuster Speakers Bureau at 1-866-248-3049 or visit our website at www.simonspeakers.com.

Manufactured in the United States of America

10 9 8 7 6 5 4 3 2 1

Library of Congress Cataloging-in-Publication Data for the hardcover edition:

Black, Michael Ian
    You're not doing it right : tales of marriage, sex, death, and other humiliations / by New York Times bestselling author Michael Ian Black.—1st Gallery Books hardcover ed.
        p. cm.
1. American wit and humor. I. Title.
    PN6165.B645 2012
    818'.602—dc23   2011038913

ISBN 978-1-4391-6786-1
ISBN 978-1-4391-6795-3 (ebook)

for martha

contents

contents

And you may ask yourself,

What is that beautiful house?

And you may ask yourself,

Where does that highway go?

And you may ask yourself,

Am I right? . . . am I wrong?

And you may tell yourself,

My God! . . . what have I done?

–TALKING HEADS, "ONCE IN A LIFETIME"

PROLOGUE

i don't know

A little while ago, I tell my wife Martha I'd like to retire.

"Retire from what?" she asks.

"All this," I say, indicating the space around me.

"The kitchen?"

"No. Just, you know, everything."

"If you retire, what will you do all day?"

"I don't know. Sit around, listen to music. Do a little writing."

"But that's what you do now."

"Oh yeah." It's true. That *is* pretty much what I do now.

"Besides, we can't afford to retire."

"Oh yeah," I say. I go back upstairs to my computer to research how much money it will take to retire. Most financial experts recommend retiring with enough money so that you continue to earn about 75 percent of your preretirement income. This is usually accomplished through a combination of pensions, Social Security, the sale of a home, dividends from investments, and finding a bag of money on the street. After running the numbers on various retirement calculators, I determine that if I need 75 percent of my average preretirement income to retire, I am off by about 73 percent. I go back downstairs.

"Maybe we should move."

"So you either want to retire or move," she says, chopping up some sort of vegetable I will soon pretend to enjoy for the sake of our children.

"Yeah."

"Where do you want to move?"

"Copenhagen."

"In Denmark?"

"Yes," I say. "Copenhagen is one of the world's best cities to live."

I know this because after researching how much money it would take to retire, I spent considerable time reading articles about the world's best cities to live; Copenhagen regularly scores quite high on these lists.

"Isn't Copenhagen cold?"

"That's actually a popular misconception. Copenhagen is temperate the entire year. January gets a little nippy, but no. Very temperate . . . good schools," I add.

"Is that what you did all day? Read about Copenhagen?"

"No."

"Did you work?"

"Of course I worked. I got a lot done."

Which is true, if you define "getting a lot done" as doing online retirement calculations, researching world's best cities to live, and spending three hours looking at photos of Britney Spears's ex-husband, Kevin Federline.

For some reason, I am mildly obsessed with Kevin Federline's weight gain, which has been substantial over the past few years. A former backup dancer, he now looks like he ate a backup dancer.

I do not know why FKF (Fat Kevin Federline) holds such fascination for me. I've never met Kevin Federline and do not know anything about him as a person, but I project onto him all the worst fears I have for myself: fear of wasted potential, fear of failure, of losing my family, of making terrible hair decisions. When I see those paparazzi images of FKF, sometimes sporting dopey cornrows, sometimes waddling across some anonymous poolside deck with beer in hand, I imagine a guy who does not know who he is, what he is supposed to be doing, or how he wound up in the unexpected circumstances of his own life. This is how I feel about myself 90 percent of the time.

I imagine FKF handles his bewilderment with food, whereas I deal with mine by searching for answers online. Which is why I decided to take an online personality test to determine if there is another career out there, one that might better suit my temperament.

The thing I was *supposed* to be doing the day Martha asked if I had gotten any work done was writing this book, a book I had been struggling with, at that point, for over a year. The book was so hard to write I thought maybe I should give up. Maybe, I thought, I need a career change, and these online personality tests will help me discover a new, more satisfying profession. Maybe if I just put my trust in the mighty Internet, all will be well.

A word of background regarding my career: At the age of nine I decided to become an actor. Most people do not follow through on the career plans they made for themselves as children. If they did, the world would have an enormous surplus of cowboys and ballerinas, and not nearly enough directors of sales for companies that manufacture ceramic floor tile. But I am one of those rare people who stuck to his childhood job plan. As a result, I have spent the last thirty years of my life living out a career choice made by somebody who had not yet mastered the ability to tie his own shoes.

Along the way, I also became a writer. In fact, the writing component of my career soon took on more importance to me than the acting. Which is how I came to be writing this book, my second. The first was called *My Custom Van . . . And 50 Other Mind-Blowing Essays That Will Blow Your Mind All Over Your Face.* That book spent exactly one week on the *New York Times* Bestseller List (#17, not that impressive), which is why I now refer to myself as *"New York Times* Bestselling Author Michael Ian Black" whenever possible. But any magic I used to have with the written word seems to be gone now. I need a new career.

Fortunately, there is no shortage of career tests on the Internet. I choose one that attempts to discern the occupation you are best suited for from a series of personality questions "based on the Jung and Myers-Briggs topology." I don't know what that means, but it sounds authoritative. Also, the word *topology* sounds like "topless," which is kind of cool.

Sample question: "You willingly involve yourself in matters that engage your sympathies. Yes or no?" That is an easy question to answer: no. Because when I am at work, that is my time to work. The workspace is not the appropriate arena for us to discuss your problems. When I am there I need to be left undisturbed to check what people are saying about me on Twitter.

Very straightforward.

But I find a lot of the questions difficult to answer. I mean, *are* my decisions based more on the feelings of a moment than on careful planning? *Is* a thirst for adventure close to my heart? I once went skydiving, which is certainly adventurous, but I cannot handle the Tilt-A-Whirl. So what does *that* mean?

The further I get into the test, the more insulted I begin to feel. How can the entirety of my personality be reduced to seventy-two yes-or-no questions? What difference does it make whether or not I prefer to isolate myself from outside noises? Which outside noises are they talking about? Jackhammers, yes. Birds singing, no. My children screaming, yes. My children laughing, yes. My children? Yes.

I write down "yes."

Although I am dubious about the accuracy of such a test, I am still excited to get my results. The test reveals that my specific personality type is known as an "INTP," which stands for "Introversion, Intuition, Thinking, Perception." And I discover that I am in very good company. Albert Einstein, Charles Darwin, and Thomas Jefferson were all INTPs. Huh. Perhaps this test is more accurate than I had originally thought. Surely, I too would make an excellent physicist, naturalist, or author of the Declaration of Independence. Excited, I scroll down to see which career the test believes would be best for me.

The answer: paralegal.

Paralegal? What the fuck? What kind of bullshit fucking bullshit is this?

You know how Burger King often employs mentally handicapped people to wipe down tables at their restaurants? What those people are to Burger King, paralegals are to lawyers. It's the lowest job you can possibly get and still technically be considered in the legal profession. Consider the following sentence I found on some random job website:

> So you're finishing college and your life plans don't extend much beyond dinner. . . . If you wanna kill some time before applying to grad school or just make enough money to avoid moving in with your parents, you should consider working as a paralegal.

That doesn't sound like a career; it sounds like a pothead. If this is the job I am best suited for, I must be the biggest loser in the world.

(Note: I am not saying all paralegals are losers. I am just implying it.)

Paralegal, however, is only the top suggestion. There are others. Like nurse and nutritionist. Both would be reasonable career choices, but I dismiss them out of hand because, as I said, I do not like hearing about other people's problems at work. Not even if doing so is my job.

Surprisingly, "novelist" appears a little farther down the list, a result I find both inspiring and upsetting. Inspiring because it seems to validate my decision to write this book. Upsetting because the fact that I am having such a terrible time actually doing the thing I am supposedly predisposed toward doing makes me think that perhaps I am incapable of doing *anything*.

Which is how I came to suggest to Martha that I retire. Surely, that is one job I could do well. As she pointed out, I was doing it already.

I recognize that retiring and moving are different iterations of the same impulse: escape. Escape from work, escape from home, escape from tedium. It is the fantasy that if I just throw the jigsaw puzzle pieces of my life into the air enough times, eventually they will come back down fully formed into a new and better image.

Not that there is anything wrong with my life. There's not. I have a great life. A wife, two kids, a house in the woods, a career at which I have found more success than I deserve. The confusing thing about it is that, oftentimes, it doesn't feel like my life at all.

Two brief examples of this phenomenon:

- I am standing in a small room at the massive Toys 'R' Us in midtown Manhattan with a sock puppet on my hand, standing beside professional soccer player Mia Hamm, former New York City mayor Rudolph Giuliani, and the Village People. We are all sharing a hearty laugh. Any other information about this incident is unimportant. What is important is that it happened, and that the weirdness of it all nearly gave me a stroke.
- I am yelling at my son and daughter to sit correctly in their chairs because it is dinnertime. The fact that they refuse

to sit correctly infuriates me because THAT IS NOT THE WAY WE SIT AT DINNER! I am suddenly unrecognizable to myself, a person who yells at other people about the correct way to sit on chairs, as if I am the snooty British judge on some terrible reality show about sitting.

I wonder if, like me, there are people who occasionally experience the curious, disembodying sensation of not recognizing their present life as their own. It is a feeling I can only describe as being the opposite of déjà vu. Rather than feeling as though you are reliving some unique moment in time, it is as if you are experiencing the mundane activities of your everyday life for the first time. So that's what this book is about, those occasional instants when I do not recognize my life as my own, and I am left wondering how I got here.

Déjà who?

Another example: When this book comes out, I will be forty years old. That fact alone is startling to me. Forty. Typed out, the word looks spindly and weird. Seriously, look at it: *forty*. It looks like a shrub that died.

Now that I'm here, I can't help but think that forty should feel different. Different how? I don't know. More serious, maybe. More competent, for sure. I never imagined after all these years I would still feel so hopelessly and radically stupid. About everything. Paying bills, fixing things, giving good advice to my children, my herky-jerky career. All manner of useful knowledge escapes me. When I hear Martha or the kids start to ask a question, I feel my stomach clench because I know the answer before they ask. The answer is, "I don't know."

"How do you change the air filter downstairs?"

"I don't know."

"What is your schedule next week?"

"I don't know."

"Dad . . . ?"

"I don't know."

How does one survive for forty years knowing as little as I do? I don't know.

At night, I read stories to my kids. Currently we are reading Laura Ingalls Wilder's *Little House in the Big Woods,* about a pioneer family in the 1800s. It is amazing to me how much those frontier people know: they kill bears and eat them, they make their own clothes, they pickle food, they mill wood. Today, if somebody *just* knows how to pickle their own food, I consider that person a genius. But pickling *and* milling? Mindblowing. I can barely survive a day with spotty Internet service.

Sometimes I worry about what I will do when the shit goes down. I'm not sure which specific shit I mean. Maybe nuclear shit or biological weapon shit or zombie shit. What if my family is cut off from civilization for an indefinite period of time and it's my job to take care of everybody? Could I muster the necessary resources to accomplish the task? I actually *do* know the answer to this question: no. When the shit goes down, my family will be the first to die.

Cluelessness is not an attractive quality in a man. Martha has long ago given up any pretense of believing in my competence. The only ones who still do are the kids. For the moment, their childish faith in my parental omnipotence remains strong. They accept my wisdom at face value, even when the answers I provide to their questions make no sense at all.

"Why is the sky blue?"

"Because starlight is the color of Smurfs."

"Why is starlight the color of Smurfs?"

"Because God's favorite color is blue."

"Why?"

"Because God is depressed."

"What's depressed?"

"Please shut up."

Right now, it's fine. They are still young enough to be oblivious to my obliviousness. But time is going by pretty fast. How long before they figure out their father is a total fraud?

When I come back downstairs again, I show Martha some photos of apartments we could rent in Copenhagen. "Don't they look great?"

"Yeah," she says, but it's clear to me from her response she is just indulging me. We're not going to Scandinavia. We're probably not even going to IKEA. We're not going anywhere. This is our home. This is our life.

The kids are in the next room playing Boggle. I hear them calling out words to each other.

"Is *xo* a word?" Ruthie yells to me. She's seven.

"*Xo?*" I say. "What's that?"

"Like when you write a letter to somebody. You put 'xo' for 'hugs and kisses.'"

"Yes," I say. "That's a word."

I go back to futzing on the computer. Martha asks what I am looking at; I show her my FKF photo collection. She studies the photo of FKF walking on the beach, gut flopping over his bathing suit, the photo of FKF draped in an oversize T-shirt eating a drippy ice cream cone. The one of FKF, Mohawk drilled onto his skull, attempting to swing a golf club. Showing her these pictures feels like letting her in on a secret; here is a man who appears as utterly inept and confused as I feel.

She doesn't get it.

"Why are you looking at those?" she asks.

"I don't know."

It's true.

I honestly don't know.

CHAPTER 1

a girl problem

She already has a boyfriend. Which should have been obvious. Girls like that *always* have boyfriends. Everybody agrees she is beautiful—and not in a "girl next door" kind of way, either. Instead, there is something about the way she carries herself and the way she looks—tall, angular, blonde—that suggests this is not a person to be trifled with. In a James Bond movie, she would be the supervillain's icy girlfriend, the one with razor blades tucked into her high heels.

Even her old-fashioned, fuddy-duddy name is attractive to me: Martha. It is a name that plays against type, a name only a gorgeous girl could make chic. If I were the kind of superficial guy who dated models, she would be the sort of girl I would be attracted to. As it happens, I am *exactly* that type of person. Unfortunately, Martha seems to have zero interest in me. And, as I said, she already has a boyfriend.

I don't learn this for a few weeks, because she is not forthcoming about her life. She is not forthcoming about anything. In fact, she rarely speaks at all. If I say hello, she will say hello, but she doesn't meet my eyes. Mostly she just sits at her desk glaring at her computer screen. Maybe she is mad at the computer. She seems kind of mad at everything. My friend Ken calls her "Smiley."

Unlike Martha, I am quite single, having most recently concluded an affair with a girl trudging through the final stages of a divorce. She is the first divorcée among my set of young artsy-fartsy New York friends, and the fact that I am sleeping with a woman who is still technically married is a huge turn-on. When we are together I constantly refer to her by her married name.

"I would like to fuck you, Mrs. Levine," I say, and for the short duration of our relationship, that is mostly what we do.

Why her marital status should prove so titillating to me I do not know. Perhaps because I had never before seriously considered marriage for myself. The whole idea of it is so remote that the act of sleeping with a married woman carries with it a fanciful, libidinous exoticism. It's like having sex with a mermaid.

Growing up, I had no reason to believe that a long-lasting, healthy marriage was even possible. Not only did my parents divorce, but every single one of their siblings did, too. Moreover, I would estimate that well over half of my friends also came from "broken homes," a phrase I have always found needlessly melodramatic:

"Have you heard? Michael's home is broken!"
"My God, how will he bathe?"

Marriage felt like a fading American institution, as relevant to me as the Elks Club. Plus, I considered myself punk rock, and punk rockers don't believe in boring societal conventions like marriage. We prefer boring societal conventions like punk rock.

I could not envision marrying any of the girls I'd dated up to that point. There hadn't been that many. I'd begun dating my previous girlfriend at the tail end of high school. After we both dropped out of college a couple of years later, we moved together into a tiny and lightless apartment in Hell's Kitchen. That lasted until she slept with a coworker, which was bad enough. Worse was my reaction, which was to spend a long night walking through a rainstorm singing Morrissey songs to myself, an image so unbearably trite it still makes my skin crawl when I think about it.

Following that breakup, I embark on my Great Year of Sexual Liberation, a year in which I devote myself to the manly art of seduction. I am determined to become a man of frequent and voracious sexual conquests. I will not become entangled in any long-term or even medium-term relationships. I will reinvent myself as the man I have always wanted to be, an unrepentant fornicator of women.

The only problem is I am terrible at it. Despite my best efforts, most nights end with me alone in my apartment, sitting cross-legged on the floor in front of the television, eating buffalo wings from a greasy cardboard box.

I don't understand: getting girls to sleep with me should be easier. At twenty-two, I have the kind of boyish good looks that are, annoyingly, most attractive to older gay men. There is even a name in gay culture for young men who look like me: "chickens." The men who pursue us are "chicken hawks."

Women don't seem to find me nearly as adorable as do fifty-year-old men in leather pants. I don't know why.

Certain friends of mine are able to pick up girls at will. I don't know how they do it. One minute, I am out with them scanning the room for potential hookups, the next they are hustling random girls into taxicabs. They aren't even necessarily the best-looking guys. They just possess something I lack. Charm, perhaps. Or swagger. Or cocaine. If a girl ever *does* throw herself at me, it is usually just because she tripped on her way to sleeping with one of my friends.

On the rare occasions when I am able to lure a comely maiden to my bed, the results are usually disappointing because I am not good at sex. I'm just not. I don't know why. It doesn't seem like sex should be that difficult. After all, the mechanics of the act are easily understood, no more complicated than "Insert Tab A into Slot B." But I cannot seem to do it right. Perhaps I am thrusting wrong, or maybe my tongue lacks proper extension—whatever the reason, it's rare that I can bring a girl to orgasm, and when I do, it feels fluky, like sinking a basketball from half court.

One time, I spend the night making out with an attractive redhead who, as morning approaches, is on top of me in her bedroom. I am attempting to bring her to climax. Despite some moaning and writhing, nothing substantive seems to be happening. Then, after a long time, just as I think I am finally making progress, just as I think all of this manual stimulation is about to pay off, she breaks from me and gently says, "Can I go to sleep now?"

Also, despite my intention to become an unrepentant

Don Juan, I cannot help but get involved with my conquests. I always give out my correct phone number. And if I should happen to spend the night with a girl, I always call the next day, whether I want to or not, which leads to many unwanted telephone conversations about their lives and problems. Girl problems are exactly the sorts of things I was trying to avoid when I began my Great Year of Sexual Liberation. No, I want to *be* a girl problem.

Another issue is that I am incapable of reading the coded language of human sexuality. There is an impenetrable semaphoric system that men and women use to communicate with each other—batted eyelashes, discreet but meaningful glances, flicks of hair. I cannot decipher these messages and so usually end up bungling flirtations. If a lady were to ever "mistakenly" drop a perfumed handkerchief near me, for example, I would probably pick it up and blow my nose into it.

The only reason I ever bed Mrs. Levine at all is that her friend relays to me the message that she finds me attractive. Otherwise, I never would have known. And for whatever reason, Mrs. Levine and I are excellent in bed together. I cannot explain it, but we are. We have nothing else in common. Our relationship consists of the following: sex, pint of Ben & Jerry's, repeat. It's perfect.

Except that I start to feel bad about myself. I start to feel, dare I say, whorish. I do everything in my power to stifle this emotion, to shrug it off as some sort of bourgeois residue from my suburban upbringing, a bit of emotional dandruff easily brushed away. But I can't. I discover I am not the person I am trying so hard to be. After a year spent seeking it, I realize I do not want carelessness.

I want a girlfriend.

So I end things with Mrs. Levine, and because I am afraid of conflict, I do it in the worst possible way. One day, without warning or explanation, I just stop taking her calls. After a couple of weeks, I hear through the same friend who set us up that Mrs. Levine is deeply hurt. She feels used. She hates me. I don't blame her. My behavior is inexcusable, cowardly, assholish.

I have finally become a girl problem.

Six months later, Martha shows up at work and I begin to wonder if my humiliating attempts to interact with her aren't karmic payback for the unfortunateness with Mrs. Levine.

I am smitten with Martha from the moment I see her. I love that she ignores me. I love that she's a bitch. Looking for any opportunity to speak to her, I show her how to play a computer game called *Minefield*. "See?" I tell her. "Your job is to find the mines without accidentally stepping on one." I try to impress her with how fast I can find the mines—really fast. It is the nerd equivalent of muscle-flexing on the beach. "Like this, see? Now you try."

"That's okay," she demurs, returning to her work. I slink away from her desk, a puppy that has just been made to smell his own mess.

Through the office ether I learn that Martha not only has a boyfriend, but she lives with the guy. He's older, around thirty, and apparently runs a hotshot film festival. *Of course* she's with some big deal jerk-off Hollywood type. That's who girls like her are *always* with.

Maybe it is the fact that she is unobtainable that allows us to become friends. Within a couple of months, Martha's chilly exterior has thawed enough so that I am able to have regular conversations with her. I learn she is twenty-five, two years older than me. She grew up in Minnesota, started college there, spent a year in Paris, came home broke, worked to save money, transferred to a college in Washington, D.C., and finally graduated the previous spring. Now she's in New York and living with her boyfriend, Christopher, who is a (self-important, phony asshole) great guy. In fact, I'd probably like him a lot, she tells me.

I'm sure I would.

One night, a friend invites me to a party for *Saturday Night Live* at one of those posh New York restaurants where nobody in New York actually eats. When we arrive, I station myself near the kitchen door to catch each waiter on his way out so I get first dibs on the yummy little meaty things on sticks. I take many.

From my satellite position on the fringes, I notice that the party seems to radiate outward from a roped-off area where I am not allowed to go. It is a party within the party, where the *SNL* cast, host, musical guest, and various VIPs hang out. Seated at a table with REM lead singer Michael Stipe are the actor Stephen Dorff, the model Famke Janssen, some other vaguely recognizable beautiful people, and Martha.

Martha? What is she doing here? And why is she allowed in the cool section? She's not cool! I'm cool! I have my own sketch comedy show on MTV! Why is she allowed in there and I'm not? God damn it. Even when I'm cool, I'm not cool.

From behind the velvet rope, I try to catch her eye. After I have been waving for a while in her direction, Stephen Dorff sees me and gives me a confused half-wave in return.

Not you, you dolt.

Finally, Martha looks over at me and whispers something to the guy next to her. He looks up. Christopher.

He's a handsome guy, but nothing special. He's not chiseled the way I thought he would be. Nor does his chin jut. I assumed he'd have a jutting chin. He's not too tan, doesn't wear bad jewelry. He just looks like a guy. Worse, he looks like a nice guy.

Martha puts her napkin on the table and joins me at the velvet rope separating us. "Hi," she says, giving me a peck on the cheek.

"Hi."

"Are you having fun?" she asks.

"Not really. Are you?"

"It's okay." After a pause, she says, "I'm so glad to see you."

"Really?"

"Uh-huh."

This is a stunning turn of events. She's "so glad" to see me? Is she drunk? I think she might be drunk. Nobody is ever "so glad" to see me unless they are drunk. Even then I suspect they are just happy to be drunk.

I do not know what to say to her in response. I point at the guy she was seated beside. "Is that Christopher?" *Why am I bringing up Christopher now? Now, when she is actually expressing interest in me? Am I stupid? Yes. I am so stupid they should put a sticker on my forehead. The sticker should read, "Warning: stupid."*

"Yeah. You should meet him."

"I can't go in there." I nod at the bouncers.

"Don't worry about it," she says, lifting the velvet rope. I duck under and follow her to the table. Nobody stops us because nobody ever stops a pretty girl. Martha introduces me to "Michael" and "Famke" and "Stephen" and, finally, to Christopher, who shakes my hand warmly and asks me some questions about myself and my TV show, but does not invite me to sit. Sure enough, he seems like a (douchebag prick star-fucker) nice guy.

Martha and I chat for a few more minutes before I find myself feeling overwhelmed by my own dullness among these luminous creatures, and I excuse myself to catch up with my friend, who has, of course, left with a girl. As I step back across the velvet divide, I glance over my shoulder. Martha's attention has returned to Christopher and the better world he inhabits. Somebody says something funny and everybody laughs. I wait for Martha to look back at me but she does not. A few minutes later, I leave the party and head home, alone, stopping on my way to pick up buffalo wings in a greasy cardboard box.

CHAPTER 2

meredith wants to give you a blowjob

Sex and work have always been intertwined for me. The first time I have any idea of the person I want to be when I grow up is when I am seven or eight years old, and my family is on a day trip from New Jersey to Washington Square Park in New York City. We're there to check out the faded site of all that jazzy sixties bohemia but the closest we get to anything resembling counterculture is watching a guy on a unicycle juggling flaming torches. When he is finished, a girl in short shorts and a T-shirt passes around a porkpie hat into which people stuff crinkly dollar bills. After she is done and the crowd has dispersed, I see him tongue kiss her as he counts his money.

This is the coolest job I have ever seen. Here is a guy who, first of all, gets to ride his unicycle to work. Second, he determines his own hours. Third, the guy is obviously making a fortune. Fourth, part of his job involves lighting things on fire. And finally, while I did not have the language to describe the highly specific envy I was feeling, I now know that what I was thinking was this: *That guy must get so much pussy.*

I want to be him when I grow up.

Eventually, I come to realize that any occupation that involves trying to get people to throw dollar bills at you is not a good job. If it were, all men would be juggling unicyclists and all women would be strippers. Maybe this is how we create these identities for ourselves, attaching tiny bits a little bit at a time, the same way plaque accumulates in our arteries and eventually kills us. Because from the moment I see that juggler, I want to move to New York and be a performer.

The second event that informed the way I thought about my future self occurred a couple of years later during my first summer at sleepaway camp. The camp was called Nah Jee Wah, a Jewish camp with an Indian name. Most Jewish camps are named for Indians. I don't know why this is, perhaps because Camp Nah Jee Wah sounds more woodsy than Camp Lipschitz.

For reasons I cannot remember, but are probably due to a lack of desire to play more kickball, I enlist in the camp play. There is a group of about fifteen of us, of varying ages and abilities. I am one of the younger kids and I am given very little to do. But I don't care. What little I have to do I love right from the get-go. We practice every day in a dim barn, and I learn what it is to be part of something grand. All these people learning to work together, it's like the army, but with dance shoes. Rehearsing that play is the best part of my summer, made even better by the presence of a girl named Meredith.

Small, freckled, and strawberry blonde, Meredith looks like a Jewish Pippi Longstocking. We bond over the fact that we are the only ten-year-olds doing the play, and because we have so little to do during rehearsal, we spend a lot of time talking. She is from Long Island. She likes horses and rainbows. She is the most fascinating creature I have ever encountered.

Soon we are spending time together outside of rehearsal, and then one day we begin holding hands, and just like that, she is my girlfriend. One hot afternoon during rehearsal, Meredith's best friend, Debbie, corners me backstage.

"Guess what?" she asks.

"What?"

"Meredith wants to give you a blowjob."

"Cool."

"Do you know what that is?"

"Yeah," I say defensively. I have no idea what that is.

"What is it then?" she asks in a challenging tone.

"It's when a girl blows in a guy's ear," I say with confidence. This seems to make sense and Debbie does not contradict me. They probably don't know what a blowjob is, either. Needless to say, nothing like a blowjob happens that summer (or for many summers after that), but over time it becomes obvious to me that Meredith wants to progress our relationship into the land of kissing.

I like her very much, but kissing seems like such a dramatic step. My kissing at that point is limited to my mother and the television screen when Molly Ringwald is on it. I do not know if I am ready to take such a dramatic step with an actual living girl. So I consult my counselor, Larry, who seems worldly because he is from England. I figure anybody with an accent that suave must know a thing or two about the ladies. I lay out the situation for him. He listens without interruption or condescension. When I am done speaking, Larry tells me to follow my heart. "And don't get her pregnant."

One night as we return from evening activity at the dining hall, I lead Meredith on a moonlit excursion around the mosquito-infested swamp we call "Lake Nah Jee Wah" to a secluded and romantic moonlit clearing beside the Dumpster. We are alone. I am nervous, both because I am going to kiss her and because bears sometimes show up there to eat the garbage. I tilt my head up toward her since she is a foot taller. I close my eyes. We kiss. On the lips, close-mouthed. She tastes wonderful, like Dr Pepper lip balm. It is just one kiss, but it is enough. When I return to my bunk, Larry asks me what happened.

"I kissed her."

"How was it?"

"Pretty good." But it was more than pretty good, and I think he can tell.

"You did okay," he says.

The play opens a few nights later. There is a moment when I am supposed to enter from backstage and make my way to the front. It is my one big moment in the musical and as I push my way downstage I trip, completely losing my balance. I feel my feet going out from under me, my body cartwheeling through the air, deep shame already building in midflight. But somehow I land upright, on my knees, and I continue on as if I meant to do it. Nobody even seems to notice. Not the audience and not my love Meredith. From my peripheral vision I see her singing and dancing beside me. She glances over at me and smiles, and I feel strong and capable, and that is the moment I know what I will be doing for the rest of my life.

We write sporadic letters to each other in the fall and winter. I cannot wait to return to Camp Nah Jee Wah to resume our romance. When summer finally comes, though, Meredith dumps me for a boy nicknamed Taco. I am heartbroken but console myself with the fact that Taco is legitimately much cooler than me. His nickname, after all, is Taco.

Even though my heart is broken, my career path is set.

Nobody at home takes me seriously when I announce my intention to become an actor. This is probably wise, since the year before I was going to play professional baseball, and the year before that I was going to be a long-haul trucker. (There was a brief, possibly drug-induced, period in the 1970s when long-haul trucking constituted the coolest career to which a man could aspire due to the song "Convoy," and various Burt Reynolds movies.) So I know that children's occupational goals can fluctuate. As I write this, for example, my nine-year-old son wants to be a roller-coaster designer. Maybe that's what he'll end up doing—the world needs roller-coaster designers—but I'm not betting on it.

I sign up for acting classes, and the following spring my mother gives me a stark choice: I can either play Little League or join the local children's theater production of the musical *Paint Your Wagon*. I cannot do both. In baseball, I am named to the all-star team two years in a row; in the play, I will be stuck in the chorus. I choose the play.

The show's lead actor is an older boy named Kurt. I am awestruck at his talent. He can sing, he can dance. He's handsome and funny, and he signifies his devotion to craft by wearing a flowy white scarf around his neck all year round. His costar is a pretty blonde named Sue who he, of course, also dates. He is my idol. After the show opens, Kurt and Sue host a big cast party at the house of one of their parents. Everybody sings along to Creedence Clearwater Revival and eats pizza. Some of the cast members make out with each other. Nobody on our Little League team ever made out with each other. Clearly I made the right choice.

Throughout high school, Kurt is always the lead in the school plays, theatrical royalty in a town that does not recognize his greatness. But I do. If anybody is going to make it, he will. He's got everything going for him: he's good-looking, he can act, he can sing, he can dance. After graduation he forgoes college in favor of New York City, Broadway bound.

He is never heard from again.

But I persist. When I am fourteen I go to theater camp, where I perform in two plays and touch my first vagina. The following winter I take classes with the camp's artistic director in New York, bundling myself onto a train for an hour and a half each way every Saturday. When the subject of college arises, I tell Mom I am going to New York University to study theater.

"What about getting a degree in education?" she asks. "That way, if acting doesn't work out you can teach."

"No," I tell her.

I am not going to be like Mr. Reilly, the lemon-faced history teacher who directs our school plays. I'm either going to succeed or I'm going to fail, but I'm not going into it with a backup plan because backup plans are for pussies.

My brother is at Carnegie Mellon in Pittsburgh, where he is studying to be an actuary, a career he chose after reading a survey in *USA Today* ranking it the best profession due to its high income and stability. Reading a chart in a newspaper seems like a random way to pick your career, but no more so than choosing one because a girl said she wanted to blow you when you were nine. (Or, for that matter, by taking an online personality test.)

I apply to NYU early decision, and the day I am accepted is the happiest I have ever had. I am going to New York. And college doesn't disappoint. I study acting and try to have sex with girls in my theater class. When we pick partners for scene study, I pair myself with an attractive classmate. Then we meet at her dorm room or mine to practice the scene. Then, hopefully, we make out. Sometimes we make out without having rehearsed the scene, which is fine, too. If I'm honest, most of the time we do not make out at all, but I choose to forget those times.

The summer after my freshman year I apprentice at the Williamstown Theatre Festival, a prestigious regional theater in the Berkshire Mountains of Massachusetts. Apprentices are the festival's worker ants, moving scenery, sewing costumes, hanging lights. We work for free in exchange for the chance to be part of a professional theater company for a season. They also offer classes and small opportunities to perform. I am a spear carrier in *Henry IV,* and a pirate (with lines!) in *Tom Jones*. When I am not working, I am attempting to seduce my fellow apprentices. Several times I miss the curtain call at the end of *Henry IV* because I am flirting with a girl backstage.

I'm not the only one for whom sex and theater are com-mingled. Actors are notoriously promiscuous. Perhaps this is because, as a breed, we tend to be attention starved. Perhaps it's because of the intense emotions our work stirs up, the long hours, the special camaraderie that develops among un-derpaid young people striving to create meaningful work. Or maybe, as I suspect, we just like to screw.

Whatever the reason, I find myself wondering if other professions are as horny. I ask my brother if actuaries have a lot of sex with each other.

"No," he says.

"What about at the Christmas party?"

"No."

"Not even sometimes?"

"It's mostly just middle-aged dudes. So, no."

Before I got married, I could not imagine spending my life going to a job where there wasn't at least a small chance of having sex with one of my coworkers. Seriously, what would be the point?

CHAPTER 3

you need to go

I should give up on Martha but I do not. This is typical of me. In all other areas of my life, I abandon whatever activity I am engaged in when it becomes difficult: guitar lessons, French class, chess, going to the gym. All of it left behind once the effort required exceeds "minimal." With girls, though, I am indefatigable. I have spent innumerable hours, weeks, and months chasing women who, despite my best efforts, remain as distant from me as the sun.

After terminating my relationship with Mrs. Levine, I spend a fruitless spring pursuing the Lovely Miss Claire Walters, a young handbag designer and first-generation Irish-American, who once made me one of the worst meals I have ever eaten— an authentic Irish plate of stringy boiled beef accompanied by tasteless boiled potatoes. It is the sort of meal Irish people sing about when they are drunk and crying. I didn't care. I told her it was delicious. I would have eaten a hundred plates of the glop just to be with her. She is a lithe little brunette thing with pale skin and moony eyes. We go out several times, although physically our relationship never progresses beyond the touching of boobs (me touching hers, not so much the other way around).

Within the first couple of weeks, it is obvious she has no real interest in me. When I suggest we get together, she tells me she has work to do at home. When I offer to hang out with her while she works, she says she does not feel well. When I offer to care for her, she tells me she is unlikely to recover. But I do not let that deter me. After all, if I gave up on every girl who had no interest in me, I would never be with any girls at all. If I just persist, I know I can get her to come around. Persistence in this case means calling at inappropriate hours, showing up at her apartment uninvited, and repeatedly asking why she does not like me more.

Eventually, the Lovely Miss Claire Walters refuses to see me or take my calls, just as I had done to Mrs. Levine. (Karma, you are indeed a bitch.) I am heartbroken, and when I take a moment to examine my stalkerish behavior in the mirror, I find humiliation and shame waving hello. Hello again, old friends, hello.

With Martha, I am determined not to allow myself to become obsessive or weird. Since she is not a legitimate possibility *d'amour,* there is no point spending all my time thinking about her, passing by her desk for no reason at all, or attempting to discern hidden messages of devotion from our every interaction. No, I will put her out of my mind. Which I do. Sort of. Not at all.

I can't help it. In addition to being a stunning-looking girl, Martha is also fun to talk to. Her initial iciness, which I first interpreted as an attractive bitchiness, was actually a brittle insecurity about being the New Girl in an incestuous work environment. Our little MTV staff has been together for three years and is populated almost exclusively by single twenty-somethings. Needless to say, a lot of discreet and not-so-discreet intramural screwing is going on. It's like *Mad Men* without the style. Any girl would feel intimidated walking into that environment. So for her first few months, Martha just glared into her computer monitor and did her best to ignore the hormonal whirlpool swirling around her. Over time, as her fear of molestation eased, she relaxed. Now she is one of the team. As such, I am hoping to molest her.

Thanksgiving is coming, and although I could go to Florida to visit my mom, I don't because Florida sucks. Instead, I plan to spend the day with my brother, Eric, who lives across the river in Hoboken. I ask Martha what she's doing for the holiday weekend. Is she going home to Minnesota? No, she can't afford it. Is she spending the day with Christopher? No, he's going to Massachusetts to be with his family. Why isn't she joining them? Because she used to sleep with his brother and it would be too awkward. Not the answer I was expecting, but okay.

She thinks she might cook dinner at Christopher's apartment for herself and some friends. Do my brother and I want to join them? We do. Don't I want to ask him first? No, he definitely wants to come.

I'd imagined that Christopher's place would be really nice. And it is. It's the sort of well-appointed Upper West Side apartment Woody Allen would put in a movie about a guy who runs a film festival. God damn you, Christopher, and your prewar crown moldings. I cannot compete with this man. I do not have, as Christopher does, a Ralph Lauren tufted leather sofa. Or hand-knotted Persian area rugs. Or forks.

Martha greets us at the door. The first word that comes to mind when I see her is *sparkly*. Has she sprinkled herself with fairy dust? I do not know, but she is almost intolerably attractive. She welcomes us into the apartment and instructs us to relax with the other guests while she finishes the turkey.

Several hours later, Thanksgiving dinner is still not ready. Martha is flustered. Apparently she has miscalculated the ratios between cooking time, oven temperature, and bird weight. I, of course, find her haplessness charming. Watching her struggle to assemble the meal is like watching a puppy fighting its way through deep snow. I offer to help, but the kitchen is small and our friend Deanna is already assisting her, which is good because I have even less idea of what to do than Martha does. Finally, around eleven, we sit down to work our way through a late meal of undercooked stuffing, cold mashed potatoes, and dried-out bird. It is one of the worst meals I have ever eaten. Worse even than the Lovely Miss Claire Walters's boiled beef and potatoes. I love it.

Martha laughs at my jokes and leans into me when she talks. Under any other circumstances, I would be convinced that there is something between us. But I do not trust my interpretation of the mysterious transmissions that pass between men and women, and I trust them even less now, especially considering the fact that I am choking down burnt turkey off her (dipshit weeny) boyfriend's Calvin Klein dishware.

After the meal, I help Martha carry plates into the kitchen.

As offhandedly as I can, I ask her what she's doing the next day.

"Nothing," she says. "What about you?"

I have no plans but I sense an opening. *What do girls like to do?* "I'm going shopping."

"What are you shopping for?"

I hadn't thought that far ahead. I say the first thing that comes to mind: "Candlestick holders."

What? Where did that come from? I don't need any candlestick holders. I have never lit a candle in my life that was not attached to a birthday cake. But girls like candles, so maybe they like candlestick holders. One of the things I learned about Martha during our talks at the office is that she was a comparative literature major. As such, perhaps she will interpret the purchase of candlestick holders as a symbolic attempt on my part to harness the inferno I sense raging between her and my girded loins. Maybe she will view me as a man who is playing with fire, as I am certainly doing in pursuing a woman who lives with her boyfriend. *Yes,* I think, *I am a man with burning passions.* Oh yes indeed, Michael, candlestick holders were a masterful choice on your part.

"Do you want to come?" I ask.

"I don't know, maybe," she says in a tone that suggests she does not fully appreciate the deep symbolism inherent in my shopping choice. (Well, what do I expect; she went to a second-tier college.) More troubling, her tone suggests to me that maybe she does not appreciate anything about my feelings for her at all.

"Whatever," I say, in a tone meant to convey that I don't care about her, either. We are just two people who don't give a shit about each other.

When she sees Eric and me out the door a little while later, she gives me her standard peck on the cheek and then asks what time she should meet me to go shopping.

"How about noon?" I ask and she says okay. Oh wow. Is this a date? No, it can't be. But maybe it is. I think this might be a date.

The next afternoon at noon I am standing on the appointed SoHo street corner waiting for Martha. I am early. She is late. Ten minutes, then fifteen. After twenty minutes, I begin wondering if she will come at all. Maybe she changed her mind. Maybe she decided going candlestick holder shopping sounded as boring to her as it would to me. Even so, I am prepared to wait all day.

Finally, I spot her loping toward me on her long legs, legs that I will one day learn she feels self-conscious about because they turn in ever so slightly at the knees. But I don't notice anything amiss with her knees. I just see the girl I like smiling at me. She doesn't apologize for being late and I don't care. She is here. She takes my arm in hers and I lead her away.

We pop in and out of various upscale boutiques, the kind that sell handcrafted Tibetan goat milk soaps and Karl Lagerfeld potpourri sachets and all manner of candle-related paraphernalia. Over the course of the next few hours, I examine and reject thousands of different candlestick holders in an effort to prolong our date as long as possible.

"Too baroque," I say about one set, even though I have no idea what *baroque* means. Hopefully, she doesn't, either.

"What's baroque about them?"

Shit. She does know. I change the subject.

Finally, after several aimless hours I settle on a pair of simple metal candlestick holders because our feet are tired and we are sick of shopping.

"What are you doing now?" I ask her.

"Nothing."

"You feel like coming over?" I ask with a clutch in my throat.

"Sure," she says.

This is totally going to happen.

We take the subway back to my place. My apartment is embarrassingly shabby compared to Christopher's. What little furniture I have is mismatched thrift store stuff, and there is a mortifying watercolor I painted of a nineteenth-century ice-skating scene on the back of my front door. It is perhaps the gayest thing I have ever done, and it is there in full view when she enters.

"What's that?" she asks.

"Oh, that's a winterscape."

"Why is it there?"

"It was like that when I moved in."

"It's horrible."

"Tell me about it."

We settle side by side on my couch and talk for a long time. About our pasts and our families and the ways in which we never felt like we fit in at home. The stuff that people talk about when they are hovering on the edge of intimacy.

Night falls. She is still on my couch. I want to kiss her but I am afraid. Does she *want* me to kiss her? I think she does, but she's got a boyfriend. Maybe the only reason she's here at all is that she knows I won't kiss her. Maybe she thinks I'm one of those "safe" guy friends. Because it's understood between us that kissing her would be wrong. It's definitely wrong, right? Or is it that I'm just a pussy and am using morality as an excuse not to make a move? I don't know what to do. Martha decides for me.

"I'm going to leave," she says.

"You are?" I ask.

"Yeah."

"Why?"

"I'm starting to feel uncomfortable."

Oh no. I blew it. I've made her uncomfortable. Can she see my hard-on through my jeans?

"Why do you feel uncomfortable?" I ask.

"I don't know what we're doing here."

I don't, either! That's the problem! What do I do? She is shifting away from me, getting ready to leave.

"Don't go," I say.

She turns back and I kiss her.

The next morning, she tells me she needs to get home. Christopher is returning from Massachusetts later in the day. I watch her pull on her jeans, slide a sweater over her body. Almost twenty years later, I still carry that image around with me—the first time I saw Martha put on her clothes. It is the sexiest image of my life. I tell her I'll take her home. Is that okay? Yes, she says. I can take her home. We ride the subway uptown to her place. I want to touch her but content myself with letting the side of my leg rest against hers during the train ride. She does not pull her leg away.

When we get to her apartment, there are half a dozen messages from Christopher on the answering machine.

"It's me," he says in the first one. "Where are you?"

In the third he says, "I'm on my way home."

By the fifth, he is calling from a pay phone, about to board a train to Grand Central Station. The sixth and final message from him says he has arrived in New York. Where is she, he wants to know, although his voice betrays no suspicion. That message came in only half an hour ago; he could be here any second.

Suddenly I am in that familiar movie scene in which the hero walks in on some jerk messing around with his girl. Everybody hates that jerk. But now *I* am that guy. Maybe I had that guy in the movies all wrong. He's not a jerk at all. He's sensitive, lovelorn. Honestly, the more I think about it, the more I realize that guy is kind of a poet.

The elevator pings a floor below. Christopher could be on that elevator. I have to get out of here. I try to leave but my lips keep finding Martha's, and hers mine.

"You need to go," she says.

"I know," I say. I don't go.

The elevator whooshes past her floor, but the next one could hold her boyfriend.

"You need to go."

She hustles me toward the stairwell. I muscle open the fire door and make my way down twelve flights of stairs to the ground floor. I poke my head into the lobby. No Christopher. As innocently as I can, I stroll across the lobby and out the revolving front door. When I am safely outside, I take a deep breath, letting the cold November air fill my lungs, still feeling her lips on mine. I should let it go. I really should. I had an amazing couple of days with the Beautiful Martha, Ice Queen of MTV. That should be enough. The wise thing to do would be to let it go and return to my Great Year of Sexual Liberation. But I do not want to, and even though the effort required to continue my pursuit of Martha will far exceed "minimal," and even though what I am doing is wrong, I want her. And I think maybe she wants me, too.

We see each other a few more times after that, but I don't know if it's going anywhere. Obviously we keep our relationship secret, and the secret makes it better. Every so often we meet at my apartment for canoodling. Oodles of canoodles. And the canoodling is very good, the way such things are when people's bodies are new to each other. At work, we ignore each other, which I find sexy as shit.

I like her. Maybe I like her a lot. But she still has Christopher. She doesn't love him, she says, but she can't afford to leave him. New York is an expensive city for a girl right out of college. If she breaks up with him, she doesn't know where she will live.

When Christmas comes, people disperse for the holidays again. This time I'm going to Florida to visit my family—my brother, sister, and mother, newly single after her nineteen-year relationship with her partner, Elaine, collapsed. So that should be fun. Ugh. I don't want to go there and spend a week consoling her about lost love. Not now when I am, for the first time in years, optimistic about my own love life. No, I want to stay here in the gusty cold city with my secret girlfriend doing secret girlfriend things (sex). Besides, my relationship with Martha is considerably better than my relationship with Christmas, a holiday I have not fully enjoyed since I was five years old . . .

CHAPTER 4

fuck you, alan alda

It's 1976. This will be our first Christmas in this other house, with these other people. We've lived here a few months now, but it still feels like we're on some crappy cut-rate vacation. The house is kind of shabby and there aren't enough bedrooms for all the kids, so I have to share one with my sister, Susan. Eric and Elaine's son, Greg, are in another. Mom and Elaine have the third; they seem to be the only ones pleased with the new sleeping arrangements.

If there is anything out of the ordinary about Mom and Elaine's relationship, I don't notice it. At five years of age, I am unable to distinguish between the various types of adult friendships—they all seem equally weird and vaguely creepy. Mom and Elaine are simply together, the way (until recently) Mom and Dad were together. The word *divorce* has yet to come up, let alone the word *lesbian*.

Nobody ever asks me to lie, but it is clear that we are not to publicly disagree with our new family's absurd cover story that Mom and Elaine are sisters. They could not look less like sisters. My mother is olive-skinned, big-bosomed, and overweight. Elaine is fair, flat-chested, and thin. They look as related to each other as me and FKF.

Conveniently, both women married men named "Schwartz," so at least we all share the same last name. The only other point of convergence is that we are all Jewish, although our Judaism is of a distinctly liberal bent. We are the kind of Jews who don't go to temple, eat a lot of bacon, and celebrate Christmas.

Jesus Christ, I love Christmas.

It is far and away the most important day on my calendar. Stripped of any devotional meaning, it is a day of naked, orgiastic greed. At five, though, my relationship with Santa is growing tenuous. Yes, I believe in him, but that belief is quietly eroding against the encroaching power of logic. Consequently, I try not to think too deeply about him. Never mind that he probably doesn't know my new address. Never mind that we do not have a chimney for him to slide down. Never mind that the gifts his elves so lovingly craft by hand in his North Pole workshop sometimes have price tags from Toys 'R' Us. Never mind that he uses the same wrapping paper Mom keeps in the basement. To question his existence is to jeopardize the appearance of the presents themselves. If Santa turns out to be fake, it could potentially upend the entire business of gift-getting. No, best to keep all thoughts on the subject to myself. To be extra safe, I should put *all* thoughts out of my mind altogether.

Later in life, when I have children of my own, I will come to hate Santa and everything he represents: forced jolliness, fuzzy logic, the exploitation of elves, children sitting on the laps of strange men. I will struggle with whether or not to preserve the Big Santa Lie and will feel enormous societal pressure to do so.

A braver man would just tell his kids the truth. "*I* bought this shit for you with *my* money and I expect you to be grateful. See? Here are the goddamned receipts. Santa my ass."

But I am not a brave man. So, as generations of parents have done before me, when Christmastime comes, I will look into my children's wide, trusting eyes and I will lie. I will feed them a line about a magic fat man and his mutant deer. And they will believe me because they are stupid.

Moreover, instead of using Santa to celebrate the holiday, I will use him as a threat. Santa will be the bad cop to my good cop.

"Personally I don't care what you do, but I would hate for *Santa* to find out you didn't put away your toys. There's no telling what that guy will do. He's crazy."

Then, having lied to my kids about one mythical creature, others will fall in line: The Easter Bunny. The Tooth Fairy. Leprechauns? Sure, why not. No wonder children are terrified of the dark. If all these mythical creatures can just come and go as they please, who's to say what else might be out there in the night?

When I was five I was scared of the dark, too, although it had less to do with supernatural beings and more to do with my sister. Sharing a room with Susan is terrifying. Every night we go to sleep and every night I think she is dead. I don't know if it's a function of her Down syndrome or what, but when she sleeps she stops breathing for long periods of time. There are often excruciating intervals throughout the night when she does not appear to be breathing at all, and I find myself lying across the room from her, wide awake in bed, reassuring myself that she is still alive.

She's fine, I tell myself. *She's fine. She's fine. She's fine.*

She's not fine. She's not breathing.

Wait.

Oh God.

She's dead.

She's dead. She's dead. She's dead.

Then, just as I am about to bolt from bed to get Mom, Susan inhales a huge, gasping breath. She sounds like a vacuum cleaner that's just sucked up a mouse. I relax. This process repeats itself throughout the night, every night.

This Christmas Eve, though, her sleep apnea (if that's what it is) becomes an asset, helping me stay awake to listen for Santa. Despite my best efforts I can't put Santa out of my mind, and I find myself seeking confirmation of his existence.

Yes, I have been warned that Santa will not come until I am asleep, but this logic seems sketchy. I mean, Christmas Eve only lasts so long; he *has* to come at some point, right? Santa wouldn't pass by our house just because one member of the household cannot fall asleep due to his retarded sister's breathing problems, right? That just seems wrong. Santa wouldn't punish all for the sins of one, would he? Not *my* Santa.

I wait. I listen. Gradually, I begin noticing that Susan hasn't taken a breath in a long time. Longer than usual. She really isn't breathing this time. I know I say that to myself every night, but this time she really isn't breathing. Every nerve in my body focuses on my sister. *Breathe!*

She's still not breathing.

Should I get Mom? I should get Mom. But what if I wake up the whole house and it turns out Susan is fine? Then *everybody* will be awake and then the Santa Rules will almost certainly apply. I don't think I can risk not getting presents just to save my sister's life.

On the other hand, Santa definitely won't come if I let my sister die. Definitely not this year and possibly never again.

She's not breathing. She's dead. I know she's dead. If she doesn't take a breath in three seconds I am going to get Mom. One . . . two . . . three . . . Nothing.

Three!

Nothing.

THREE!

Oh my God, I think she might actually be dead this time. Presents or no, I need to get Mom. I wriggle out from underneath my blanket and tiptoe into the hallway. When I do, I hear noise coming from downstairs.

Santa?

Monster?

My ears strain toward the sound, trying to determine its origin. I dare not move. If I move, the floor might creak. If the floor creaks, whoever is downstairs, Santa or monster, will discover me. From the spot where I am rooted, I can just see a sliver of the living room. Something is down there. I am terrified.

A flash of movement below. What is that? Something being held aloft. It looks like a present, being carried by whom, or what, I cannot say. But it doesn't look like Santa. All I see is a snatch of blue the exact color of Mom's robe.

From behind, I hear Susan take an enormous, raking breath. I had completely forgotten about my dead sister. I rush back into bed and close my eyes in case somebody comes to check on her. But nobody does.

Then, I don't know what happened, but it is morning and all of us boys are up with the sun and hurling ourselves down the stairs into the living room. There, scattered around the base of our very natural-looking plastic Christmas tree, is a gorgeous, glistening mound of presents.

HE CAME! I don't know when the son of a bitch did it, but he came. I love you, Santa. I never doubted you for an instant.

We are forbidden from opening anything until Mom and Elaine come downstairs, so we stand back and admire our bounty. I circle the tree's circumference, picking my name out among the gift tags. There are presents for me from Mom and Eric and Susan, one from Elaine and Greg, and in the middle, an enormous box whose gift tag reads, "To Michael. From Santa."

My God. It is far and away the biggest present of all, which means, of course, that it is far and away the best present of all. I have heard the expression that good things come in small packages, but that saying has always struck me as a vicious lie, something people say to comfort those who have just received a pair of socks. The best presents are big. Model railroad sets. Big Wheels. Electric-powered cars you can actually drive. It is obvious to me and every child I know that a present's size is directly proportional to its greatness. This year, the biggest, most obviously awesome present is for me. And it is from Santa. There is only one conclusion I can draw from this unexpected turn of events: Santa is real and he loves me best.

I am truly a magnificent little boy.

Finally—*finally!*—Mom, Elaine, and Susan come down-stairs and we are granted permission to open our presents. Although I am dying to know what's in the big box, I do not open it. I am going to save it for last, and when it is time, I will tear off the wrapping paper half an inch at a time, drawing out the suspense as long as I possibly can. This is how a five-year-old cock-teases himself.

We rip through our presents: board games (so-so), puz-zles (boring), clothing (boring, the worst), a Barbie for Susan (boring), baseball cards (cool), SnapTite automobile models (pointless: they will never be assembled), a record album of silly songs (hilarious: includes the song "Disco Duck"), picture books (boring), balsa wood airplanes (good: will not survive the day), and then whatever boring shit the grown-ups got.

In about ten minutes, the magnificent pile beneath the tree is gone, replaced by a debris field of torn wrapping pa-per, crushed cardboard, and crinkly shards of cellophane. All that remains to open is my giant Santa Box, standing tall and proud alone among the ruins.

I drag the box out and place it in front of me. I tap it to get a sense of its heft. Substantial. All eyes are on me. Perhaps I should give a speech.

"Open it already," Mom says.

Instead of peeling off the paper one tiny strip at a time as I had planned, I dig my nails under the tape seams and yank as hard as I can. The paper falls away like snakeskin, revealing a colorful cardboard box. On the box is a picture of a girl about my age engaged in some happy activity. What is she doing? What is this?

WHAT IS THIS?

I do not yet know the phrase "What the fuck?" but that is what I would say if I knew the words. Instead I just stare, mute, horrified.

It is an Easy-Bake Oven.

How could this happen? Months earlier, I had *specifically* written a long list of items I needed from Santa, and I distinctly remember that "stupid fucking girl's toy" was not on that list. And then, all at once, I make two realizations. The first is that there is no Santa. The second is that my lesbian mother is trying to turn me gay.

Well, *gay* isn't the right word because I don't know that word at age five, nor do I really think that's the case. But instinctively, I understand that the gift represents something larger for my mom, that her gift to me is as much a political statement as it is a Christmas present.

Since she and Elaine have gotten together, my mother has changed. Obviously, she is now banging the neighbor lady, which is new, but I mean my mother is undergoing some quiet metamorphosis. She used to be a mom-mom, the kind of mom that stays at home and packs lunches and stores coupons in a special avocado green coupon box purchased at a Tupperware party.

There is less of that now. She is still my mom, still loving and supportive. But she's also harder. There's an edge to her now. She and Elaine smoke Virginia Slims. They read (or at least subscribe to) *Ms.* magazine. The word *feminist* begins creeping into daily conversation, a word I vaguely understand to mean "men are assholes." My comprehension of the word will expand over time, and as I grow older, I will come to think of myself as a feminist, but at the time it feels like an angry word, often accompanied by the phrase "male chauvinist pig." Although I never understand exactly what turns a man into a male chauvinist pig, I am pretty sure it's a penis.

The solution to all this porky male chauvinism is to create gender equality. How do you create gender equality? By creating New Seventies Man. New Seventies Man is tough but sensitive: equal parts hunter-gatherer/cupcake-maker. He plays baseball, yes, but only on coed Little League teams. He does not join the Boy Scouts because the Boy Scouts are, as my mother once tells me, "a sexist organization." New Seventies Man loves Lily Tomlin. He cries often, and is not afraid to express his fears, but he certainly does not run screaming into the street in his underwear after the doctor tells him he needs to get a shot, as I have recently done.

Does New Seventies Man think a breastfeeding mother is the most beautiful sight on earth? He does. Does he wish that he himself could lactate so he could relieve his partner's burden? Oh yes. New Seventies Man is respectful and kind and deferential. And lest you think no such man exists, I am here to say you are mistaken. There is such a man.

His name is Alan Alda, and he is the only man on earth with whom Mom and Elaine can find no fault. (Alan Alda, if by some miracle you are reading this book, there is something I have been waiting thirty-five years to say to you: Fuck you.)

This is the man I am expected to become. Of course, as a child, I cannot articulate this intuitive sense I have about my mother's expectations for me any more than I can speak Latin, but I feel it deep within my shitty male XY chromosomes. So I just stare at the Easy-Bake Oven with an offended expression on my face.

"What's the matter?" Mom asks. "Don't you like it?"

NO! NO! NO! No, I don't like this stupid pink plastic thing. No, I don't like living in this stupid house with these stupid people I barely know. No, I don't like being a pawn in your feminist social experiment. No, I don't like sharing a room with my retarded sister who doesn't even know how to breathe right. No, I don't like this new life and I want it to stop.

"I like it," I say.

She is not convinced. "I thought you wanted an Easy-Bake Oven."

This is typical of my mother. She invents other people's opinions for them. "I thought you loved plaid," she might say. When you ask her why she thinks you love plaid, she will lie: "You told me you *love* plaid." If you tell her you never said that, she will get mad and insist you are mistaken. "You love plaid," she will say again, as if repetition will make it so. "You love it."

Although I am choking on my rage, I agree that yes, I must have at some point demanded that Santa bring me the most effeminate toy his little elves can make. Perhaps he could also wad up a pair of pink panties for my stocking to complete the humiliation I feel under Eric's and Greg's mocking gazes.

But I feel like I can't reject the gift because to do so would be to reject the new, postpenile worldview Mom and Elaine are attempting to construct. Doing that would be the same thing as rejecting her. I can't do that. I still depend on my mother to pour my cereal.

More than that, I just don't want to hurt her. She seems happy, or at least happier than she was with my dad. When they were together, they were always screaming at each other. I remember coming downstairs during one of their arguments and seeing them yelling at each other across the dining room table like chained dogs trying to kill each other, their faces strained and purple. Dad left home several times and didn't come back for days. Now there is at least peace, although over time that peace will wear away as Elaine's own emotional issues become evident.

That night, all of us boys sit down at the kitchen table with Mom and shake envelopes of dusty brownie mix into the little petri dishes that came with the Easy-Bake Oven. We add water, stir, and watch through the oven door as a sixty-watt lightbulb transforms the watery goo into tiny chocolaty desserts. They come out brown and soft and good smelling. How do they taste? I would be lying if I said they taste anything other than delicious. I hate them and everything they represent, but they are fantastic lightbulb brownies.

We eat our treats and go to bed, another Christmas crumpled up like so much wrapping paper. That night, I lie in bed listening to my sister not breathing, and I think about that watery sludge turning into brownies, and about how quickly one thing can be changed into another.

The next day, the Easy-Bake Oven gets shoved into the closet, never to reappear. When holiday season rolls around again, I tell my mom I want a Big Wheel.

"Tell Santa," she says.

"I'm telling *you*," I respond.

That Christmas, a Big Wheel shows up under the tree with a card that reads, "To Michael. Love, Mom."

"Do you like it?" she asks me.

I tell her I do, and this time I mean it. Then I ask Mom if I can take it for a test drive. And even though it is well below freezing outside, she lets me go.

CHAPTER 5

i love you two

Things with Martha are easy and sexy and fun. We are just having a thing, fooling around. When we see each other it's great, and when we don't it's no big deal. At least that's what we tell each other. But the truth is, our early relationship is never as carefree as I pretend. I am falling in love with her almost from the moment we meet. But it's stupid to even admit that to myself for all the obvious reasons. Plus I don't want to scare her off, the way I did with the Lovely Miss Claire Walters. For now, I will try to content myself with our unserious affair. I never ask her to break up with Christopher and she does not ask me to stop seeing other girls. Of course, there aren't many other girls.

But there is one.

A recurring fantasy I have as a young man is that I will meet a beautiful girl at the Metropolitan Museum of Art. Why there, I do not know since I do not particularly enjoy going to art museums and of all the art museums in the city, I like the Met least of all. It's just a big, joyless stone box where dead people are venerated, more mausoleum than museum. Nevertheless, it is the Met where my fantasies reside and it is the

Met where I go when I am in my twenties, bored, and on the prowl. Although I like art, I have no passion for it. My passion is for girls who like art.

The best galleries for girl watching are the Impressionist rooms on the second floor. If there is one thing I know about Impressionist paintings, it's that they totally make girls wet. All those soft, blurry pastels, all those dreamy landscapes. Girls like to lose themselves in Degas's ballerinas, Renoir's bathers, Pissarro's landscapes. It's all very lovely and ethereal and gooey-girly. A perfect place to catch the eye of a winsome, bohemian art lover, but one who shaves her armpits.

I never met anybody. Admittedly, a lot of that was my fault because I never talked to anybody. But in my fantasy, she started the conversation, not I. Because if I start the conversation it just looks like I'm some creepy dude on the make. Which I am. But I don't want to *look* like that. The way it would work is that I would be staring up at a painting, hands locked behind my back in a manner suggesting deep, focused concentration. She would approach, probably wearing glasses, probably carrying a sketch pad under her arm. After a few contemplative silent moments together, she would speak: "Those water lilies are so impactful."

"Yes," I would respond. "Monet really painted the shit out of water lilies."

Then we would go back to her (tastefully appointed, well-lit, cockroach-free) artist's garret and fuck.

That is the fantasy. But like most fantasies, it does not come true. Until it does. It's a Saturday. I am at home in my little apartment with nothing to do. The week before I had bought a sleazy red leather jacket on the street for twenty dollars. I like it because it makes me look like heroin-era Lou Reed, and I am thinking, *Maybe if I wear my jacket to the Met some girl who finds heroin-era Lou Reed attractive will also find me attractive.* So I put on my sleazy jacket and head uptown.

I don't know if there is a real lack of Velvet Underground fans at the mausoleum that day or what, but nobody says a word to me, not even the Japanese who can reliably be counted on to ask me to take their picture. After a couple hours I am bored, my feet hurt, and my jacket is making me hot. I am making my way toward the exit when I hear a voice call, "Michael?"

I turn.

It is a girl. More than that, it is a beautiful girl. No glasses, no sketchbook. But blonde and beautiful.

"Hi," I say.

"Hi. I was at your taping last night."

"Oh yeah?" I ask because I am a sparkling conversationalist in the presence of beauty.

"Yeah. My roommate knows Ben from Tennessee." Ben is a guy in our sketch group; this opens up a whole avenue of possible conversation about the fact that Ben and I dropped out of college in order to tour the country together as Teenage Mutant Ninja Turtles. I can already envision Katie and I sitting across from each other at a diner languidly turning the spoons in our coffee mugs as I regale her with stories from life on the road as Raphael, the brooding ninja turtle with the red headband.

"Cool," I say.

Silence.

"Okay, well I just wanted to say hi," she says. God she's cute.

She stands there for a second with a smile on her face, obviously alone. She probably just came here by herself to see the Impressionists. But then she ran into me, the cute guy she just saw making a popular TV show the night before. This must be very exciting for her. We're totally going to do it.

"Bye," she says.

"Bye."

I watch her walk through the museum's big glass and gold doors and into the sunlight. *Don't go!* I am screaming in my head. But she's gone. I am such an idiot. Why didn't I get her number? Why didn't I ask her out? This is exactly why I can't have nice things!

When I get back home I call Ben and ask him if he knows the roommate she was talking about. He thinks so. She's a freshman at NYU. A freshman? Which would mean the girl I met is only eighteen or nineteen years old. I'm not sure how I feel about that. Actually I am sure, but I am pretending not to be because it would be unseemly to admit how much the words "barely legal" turn me on. Can he call her and get the roommate's name? He promises he will. Now? Sure, sure. It takes days of pestering before he finally gets around to it, almost as if getting me laid isn't the most important thing in his life. Finally he gets me her name and number.

I call.

"Hello?"

"Hi, is this Katie?"

"Who's this?"

"Yeah, hi, this is Michael Black . . ."

Silence.

"We met at the art museum the other day?"

"Oh yeah . . . hi."

"Yeah. Hi. Good."

Long silence.

"So, I was wondering if you wanted to maybe get together sometime for dinner or something?"

Silence.

"But *not* at the student cafeteria." God, I'm smooth.

Silence.

"Okay."

You're damned right okay! We arrange to meet a couple nights later at a casual place near her school. I wear my sleazy red leather jacket again. I have no idea what she wears because I only pay attention to girl's outfits insomuch as they relate to how far I can see down their shirts.

During my Great Year of Sexual Liberation, I have learned the secret to a good first date: Ask a lot of questions. It's a good strategy because most people love talking about themselves. I know I do; in fact, I am currently writing a book in which I do nothing but that. On my first date with Katie, I dig out all the pertinent first-date dish. She is a nineteen-year-old college freshman from Indiana. She has two brothers whom she loves very much and two parents she adores. She loves animals, especially chimpanzees. Katie is as fresh and wholesome as a squirt of fresh milk from a cow's teat.

And like fresh milk, she is kind of a bore.

Plus I am four years older than her. Not a huge age difference, but I have already been living a fully adult life for those four years. This girl just seems so young to me. *Too* young? Too innocent? Too boring? Ordinarily I would say yes except for one simple, yet important fact: She is *so* hot.

After our meal, we wander back to her place and she invites me up. Her "place" is a dorm at NYU, the concrete warehouse where they store freshmen. I feel stupid signing in to a dorm. Does the security guard know that my interest in this girl is only prurient? That I am only interested in sullying this doe-eyed young creature? If so, he does not say anything. But I feel bad. I feel bad getting into the elevator and I feel bad listening to her chatter on about the wonders of Indiana. I feel bad because she is so nice and clean and all I want to do is finger her.

I should leave. I should definitely leave.

We get to her room. The front door is, of course, decorated with construction paper cutouts of stars with each girl's name written on them in glitter glue. God, I feel dirty.

What is going to happen here? What are we going to do in this place that smells like industrial disinfectant and Secret underarm deodorant? As it turns out: nothing.

When we walk in, her roommate from Tennessee is at her desk studying. Well, that's just bullshit. Unless it's about to get kinky really fast, this date is not going to progress the way I want.

Katie introduces us. We chitchat for a few minutes. Great to meet you, so you and Ben went to the same high school, that's so amazing, canyoupleaseleaveI'mtryingtofingeryour roommate, yeah New York *is* a lot of fun. Some boys from the hall knock on the door. Can they hang out? Sure! Let's all hang out together! You, me, Katie, her roommate, the Boy Scouts, and the Mormon fucking Tabernacle Choir.

I give it one unbearable hour and then I bid my good-nights. At the door to her room, Katie presents a cheek, which I kiss. "That was really fun," she says.

"Yeah," I say. "We should do it again."

"I'd like that."

"I'd like that, too."

I wouldn't like that. Why am I saying I would like that? Why did I just make another date with this girl? Am I that hard up? Yes. Yes, I am. I am fuming all the way back to my grown-up apartment where I live alone because I am a grown-up.

A couple of nights later, we go out again. It is exactly as before. She blathers on about her mom and dad and all the great people from where she comes from—Indiana, by the way—and she has no idea that most people do not float through life on a taffeta-covered parade float because most people do not look like her. *Please put out,* I am thinking. *This will all be worth it if you just put out.*

She does not put out.

Why am I so attracted to these fresh-faced maidens? They are not looking for what I am looking for. They want boy-friends and hand-holding and breathless diary entries. I want to experiment with anal. Why don't I go for sluts and drunks? I should end it with Katie but I can't bring myself to do it because she's so—and I hate to use this mealymouthed word but sometimes it is the perfect descriptor—nice. God, she is so nice.

My relationship with Martha starts a couple of months after I meet Katie. I do not tell Katie about Martha, but I *do* tell Martha about Katie. It turns me on to talk to her about this other girl I'm seeing. It turns me on to say unkind things about her, to say she's boring, to laugh at her prudishness and unabashed enthusiasm for the world.

One night just before the holidays, a musician friend of mine is playing a show downtown. Everybody I know is going to be there. I am going with Katie, Martha with Christopher. It's hot, the place is mobbed, people are bumping against each other. Half an hour into the show, I am standing with Katie near the bar. I've seen Martha and Christopher earlier in the night, but I do not know where they are. Then I feel hands on my waist, hands sliding down to my ass. It's Martha. Katie is in front of me and does not see anything.

That night, when I drop her off at the dorm, Katie gives me a small wrapped box. A Christmas present. I do not know what to say. I haven't gotten her anything. She says that's okay, she just saw this and thought I would like it. I open it up there in the hallway. It's a coffee mug from the World Wildlife Fund with a photo of a baby chimpanzee on it.

I hate it.

"Oh wow," I say. "I love it."

She beams and kisses me, long and slow, opening my mouth with her pale nineteen-year-old tongue. It's a different kiss than the mannered ones we've shared before. Before, she was always holding something back. But not now. There's an urgency to it. She presses against me as we kiss, filling the crevices of my body with her own.

"Do you want to come over?" I ask her. She doesn't answer right away.

"When I get back from break, okay?"

I can tell what's happening: she wants to sleep with me and is trying to convince herself it's okay. If I can just wait until after winter break, I can finally have sex with her and then, in all likelihood, dump her.

When I get back to my apartment I call Martha.

"Can you come over?"

"No." She's with Christopher and can't talk. She hangs up.

I don't tell Martha that I bought her a Christmas present. It's a small wooden chess set because she said she wanted to learn. I've got it in my bedroom, wrapped and waiting for her. I hold my new coffee mug in my hand and look at that stupid baby chimpanzee and feel lonely and sorry for myself and horny. Mostly horny.

While I'm in Florida I think a lot about what I am doing with Katie. The more I think about her the worse I feel. I can't do to her what I did to Mrs. Levine. Katie is too young. Too earnest, as clean and transparent as a sheet of plastic wrap. Hurting her the way I did Mrs. Levine would be too awful and I do not want to be an awful person. Especially because I think she is falling in love with me. And why not? I am older, more worldly, smart, zitty. (Admittedly the "zitty" part might not be as much of a turn-on.)

I think about Martha, too, and how much I care for her. How I don't think I can keep sharing her. How maybe I'm falling in love with her. And why not? She's a little older, more worldly, smart, not zitty.

And what I am to Katie, and Martha is to me, maybe Christopher is to her.

Ugh.

My first call when I get back to New York is to Martha.

"I want to see you," I say. She is noncommittal.

"I don't know," she says. "Maybe in a few days."

Why a few days? Wasn't she thinking about me the same way I was thinking about her? Did she rethink our relationship over the holidays? Are we through? Did she choose Christopher over me? I think that's probably what happened. She had a few weeks to think about what we were doing, decided she had to pick, and she picked Christopher. Of course she picked Christopher. I would pick Christopher over me, too. He's a (pretentious starfucker) great guy. This is awful.

Thank God I still have Katie waiting in the wings. Katie's not so bad. She's just a little young, that's all. So she's a little boring. So what? I'm sure not everything that comes out of my mouth is so fascinating, either. So what if we don't have that much to talk about. Soon we will be sleeping together and that will make everything right between us, right? She gave me her phone number in Indiana before she left two weeks ago. I call her, the first time I've used the number.

"Hello?"

"It's Michael."

"Hi!" she says. She is so bright and chipper. She sounds like she just came in from a horse-drawn sleigh ride.

We talk about our holidays. Mine were miserable. My mom was miserable. We mostly just sat around watching daytime television with my brother and sister, Florida is wretched, etc. Hers were fantastic. She had an amazing time with her family. They tobogganed and sang carols, Indiana is so beautiful this time of year, etc. Listening to her talk about her time at home with her good, happy family, I realize the problem isn't her. It's me. I'm the asshole. I'm the one who can't even see an amazing girl when she's waving her pom-poms right in my face. If I could just get some of her old-fashioned Midwestern pep to rub off on me, we could be a great couple. That's how people would describe us, too, as "a great couple." I can't wait for her to get back to New York. We don't even have to have sex right away. We can even wait until marriage if she wants. This is going to be great!

"Listen," I say. "I can't see you anymore."

"Oh." Her voice goes kind of flat.

"I started seeing somebody else and I don't feel right seeing both of you at the same time . . ." I trail off.

"Oh . . . okay." There is a long pause. "Well, thanks for calling."

"Yeah."

"Happy New Year."

"You, too."

I hang up. I make a cup of tea and drink from the mug she gave me. I turn on the TV and watch the Knicks. They're losing. When the game is over I sit in the dark for a while. I live on the twenty-sixth floor. There's another building directly across the street and when the sun goes down, I like to stare into the lives of all those people, or at least the ones who do not close their shades. There are a lot of young families over there, a lot of single professionals, a lot of old people, both alone and in couples. I'm not looking for anything weird; I just like to watch them sometimes. A little while later, the phone rings. It's Martha.

"I want to see you," she says.

CHAPTER 6

engaged

A few weeks later, Martha breaks up with Christopher. No more secrets. No more sneaking around. We hold hands and make out on subway platforms. Our relationship flowers. We are in love. I want to spend every second with her. A year into our bliss she asks if she can move in with me. I tell her no fucking way.

At the time, she is sharing a musty uptown apartment with a very shy, very short African-American volleyball player who is also a hunchback. I know that sounds like a joke, but it is not. She found the place after answering a classified ad he'd taken out in the *Village Voice*. He seems like a decent guy, but I never get to know him well because whenever I am there he retreats to his bedroom and quietly shuts the door. The only time I am ever in his bedroom he shows me all his volleyball trophies, which line the room's entire perimeter. How a tiny hunchback *won* so many volleyball trophies is never explained to me. Maybe there is a tiny-hunchback volleyball league. I don't know.

(Also, for some reason her apartment always smells like lentils. Lentils are an okay smell, but given the choice between *always* smelling lentils or *never* smelling lentils, I choose never.)

Our living arrangement works great for me, but for Martha it is a minimum half-hour subway commute each way, an hour of extra time every few days when she needs clean clothes and to refresh the contents of her makeup bag. Eventually she grows tired of it.

"We should move in together," she says one day. It is a conversation I'd been expecting and dreading.

"I like living alone," I say.

"But we're here every night, anyway," she says. Then she starts enumerating all the reasons why it "makes more sense" for us to live together: it would be fun and easier and we would get to spend more time together, and more than anything, because she loves me. She is so full of shit.

I mean, I do believe that she loves me but that's not why she wants to move in together. She wants to move in with me because I have a rent-controlled apartment, which is New York City's greatest and rarest treasure. Having a rent-controlled apartment in New York is like living in medieval Europe and having spices.

"I really like living alone," I repeat.

The last couple years have been the first time in my life that I've lived alone. I love it. Even though Martha and I really do spend most of our time together, having my own place means knowing that at any moment of my choosing I can ask her to get the hell out, and she will have to do it, as once happened when I walked in on her reading my journal. "Please leave," I said. And she did. It won't be so easy to press the eject button if all her stuff is here, at least without the manual labor involved in packing her things. If there is one thing I hate more than lost love, it is manual labor.

"Maybe I could just move in for a little while," she says.

"Yeah, but if you do that, you'll just end up staying."

"I wouldn't do that."

"I don't think it's a good idea."

"Just for a little while."

"No."

She moves in the next month.

"Temporary," she says.

Neither of us believes her. At first, Martha makes a few halfhearted attempts to find her own space. An apartment becomes available across the street: too collegiate. There is one down the block: too cramped. She looks at a few others but nothing is good enough. She is Goldilocks and I have the only bed in New York City that feels just right.

To my surprise, cohabitation works out okay. As much as I loved having my own space, I also love finding her there when I come home, or hugging her when she comes home to me. Now, two years later, I sit cross-legged across from her on the floor of our apartment trying to figure out exactly how I am going to propose.

The idea of marriage begins, as every relationship idea does, with Martha. She is twenty-eight, around the age when women first begin contemplating their reproductive mortality. I am two years younger, around the age when men are not generally contemplating much of anything. It starts as a bit, a routine she and I do as a kind of verbal punctuation mark to any happy, shared experience. Like maybe we are walking back from one of our regular strolls down Third Avenue to Ben & Jerry's. As we walk, she might take my hand and sigh and press her shoulder against me and say, "Will you marry me?"

Whenever she says that I squeeze her hand and say something like, "Yes. Yes I will marry you, my sweet. We will marry and spend the rest of our days exactly as we are now, arm in arm, filled with Chunky Monkey." But I don't mean it. Not really. And I don't think she means it, either.

After a year of those happy sighs, though, I start to wonder: Maybe she's serious. Does she *really* want to get married? I mean, I think she probably wants to get married *eventually,* start a family *eventually.* But not now. Surely she cannot mean now. I am content to keep everything on its present course. But I cannot keep ignoring those little sighs of hers. Over time, I am forced to conclude that when she says, "Will you marry me?" she is not being metaphorical. She actually wants to get married.

Do I?

Shit. I don't know.

After reasoning through the problem to the best of my ability, I come to several conclusions, which lead, one after the other, to my ultimate decision:

- I love her and do not want to break up with her.
- Nor do I imagine us breaking up in the foreseeable future.
- She is the first person I have ever envisioned myself marrying.

- Despite all evidence to the contrary, I still like the idea of marriage even though I cannot explain why.
- If I can envision marrying her, perhaps I should marry her. One day. Not now.
- If I believe I am going to eventually marry her one day, why not marry her now? The only reason not to would be that a part of me believes somebody better might come along, and if I really believe that, then the right thing to do would actually be to break up with her now, which I do not want to do, thus taking me back to the top of my "logic ladder™" (a term I have just invented, and am in the process of trademarking).

But logic does not feel like a good enough reason to get married. Marriage is an emotional act as much as a rational one. My emotions aren't there yet. As I am thinking about all this, a quiet mantra begins to insert itself into my brain. I am almost embarrassed to admit that this happened, but it did. In the weeks leading up to my decision, I start hearing a voice. It is an actual voice speaking to me from someplace at the back of my brain. This is what the voice says: *Choose hope over fear.* I hear the voice all the time, the same four words again and again.

Needless to say, the voice sounds a lot like Oprah.

I am at a loss to explain the voice in my head. I am not a religious person and do not believe the voice has any religious significance. Nor am I a regular viewer of *The Oprah Winfrey Show.* But the voice is there nonetheless, quiet and unyielding. *Choose hope over fear,* it insists.

It is two days before Christmas, three Christmases after I first realized I was falling in love with her. We are leaving for her parents' house in Minnesota the following morning and have decided to open our presents before we go so that we do not have to lug gifts back and forth. When we are done opening presents—books, girly soaps, a sweater, a couple of CDs—Martha looks at me and quietly asks, "Isn't there something else?"

She knows.

I was worried about this. A few weeks ago, I stupidly left the computer on one day while researching diamonds on the Internet. I went out to run an errand, and when I returned she was home, the computer still on a Web page listing the Four C's of diamond buying (color, cut, clarity, carat). She didn't say anything about it, and I wasn't sure whether she even saw the monitor. But I was pretty sure she did. Because she sees everything.

"Yes," I say. "There's something else."

Her eyes widen.

"I ordered that food processor you wanted, but it's late." This is true. I really did buy her the Cuisinart she wanted; it's late because I didn't order it on time.

"Oh," she says and straightens her face into a smile. "Thank you." She kisses me.

"You're welcome. Merry Christmas."

I then excuse myself because I have hidden her engagement ring in the bedroom. Also, I feel a severe case of diarrhea coming on.

Earlier that night, I'd asked her what she wanted for dinner.

I wanted to make the night special, but I didn't want to tip my hand, suspecting that she already knew I was going to propose. Rather than make reservations at some hoity-toity restaurant, I just casually offered to take her wherever she wanted to go.

"You know what I want? KFC," she said.

"Really?" I asked. "Because we could probably go someplace a little nicer."

"No. I'm in the mood for KFC."

My marriage proposal was preceded by a three-piece order of regular crispy, mashed potatoes with gravy, and two biscuits. Utensil of choice for the most important night of our lives: the spork.

Now that the moment is upon me, the combination of nerves and four thousand calories of secret herbs and spices is exacting a very specific toll on my body in the form of what I will delicately refer to as an "ass geyser."

After a painful and rather effluvial half hour, I sneak into our bedroom to retrieve the ring. Martha is still in the living room when I return, the ring box hidden behind my back. How to do this? The whole "on bended knee" thing has always struck me as kind of corny. Who am I, Sir Lancelot? Instead I just sit down beside her and present the box. Inside is the one-carat, classic-cut, "Tiffany style" platinum diamond ring I ordered from the Internet.

(Yes, I ordered my wife's engagement ring off the Internet because it was so much cheaper than Tiffany's. I think Tiffany's is such a rip-off. I hate that place. It is, of course, Martha's favorite store.)

"You know what? There was something else," I say, presenting the ring. I don't know how else to say it, so I just say it: "Will you marry me?"

She takes a deep breath and gives the answer every man wants to one day hear: "I don't know."

I am overjoyed. Wait. What? What did she just say?

"I don't know," she stammers, "I just need to think for a second."

She needs to think? Think about what? For a year now she's been saying she wants to get married. "Mmm, ice cream, let's get married." "Yay. We're having sex. Let's get married." "This is a good TV show. Let's get married." Now I'm proposing and she needs to think about it? What the fuck?

Maybe I really did catch her off guard. Maybe she didn't see the diamond information on the computer screen. Maybe this is all a complete shock to her. Maybe I just made a huge mistake.

Finally, after what feels like a long silence, she says, "Yes."

"Yes?"

"Yes, I'll marry you."

But now I'm a little freaked out.

"Are you sure?"

"Yes."

"Because it seems like maybe you're not sure."

"I'm sure. Yes."

"Because if you're not sure . . ."

"Yes!"

She's sure. We're getting married. I leap on top of her and kiss her on the hardwood floor.

"Ow," she says. "You're hurting my back."

We wait until the next morning to start calling people. Our friend Kerri, my mom, her childhood BFF, Kaela. We tell everybody except her mom and dad since we are arriving there in the morning and figure it will be more fun to tell them in person.

Her parents pick us up at the Hubert Humphrey Airport and drive us to the fading *Brady Bunch*–style suburban split-level they've lived in for thirty years. Martha's parents are good people, but they are Minnesotans, descended from the chilly people of northern Europe. They do not know how to express emotion and rarely talk about anything beyond the local sports teams or the weather.

When we arrive at the house, we assemble in the foyer to shed our coats and boots. Her parents are there, her younger sister is there, the dog is there, jumping on everybody. Everybody yells at the dog. Martha and I make eye contact. There's too much bustle. Clearly this is not the best time to make our announcement.

Martha says, "Guess what? We're getting married!"

A moment of flustered silence follows. Even the dog seems a little unsure what to do. Then her mom says, "Oh! Well . . . ," letting the word *well* dangle into infinity. It is not disapproval in her voice, exactly. I don't know what it is. Surprise, maybe. Not the good kind. The kind where the doctor says you might need some more tests.

Then her dad says, "Congratulations!" and seems to mean it. He gives Martha a big hug and shakes my hand. Thin-lipped Norwegian smiles all around. We stand awkwardly in the foyer for a few more seconds until he says, "Boy, it's cold out there."

Then we talk about the weather for twenty minutes.

I can see Martha is crestfallen. I know she wanted her parents to be more excited for her, to compliment her ring (indistinguishable, by the way, from an *actual* Tiffany ring), for her mom to talk about dresses and arrangements and all the gossipy plans women make the minute a wedding is announced. But that doesn't happen. Instead her dad and I silently watch the Vikings on TV while her mom bakes a hot dish (Minnesotan for "casserole") in the kitchen, and Martha pretends not to mind their indifference.

I feel bad for her. I want her happiness teased out to endless lengths. I want her congratulated for making such a fine choice in a husband. We are high on hope for our own futures and want others to catch our buzz. When that does not happen, it's a total killjoy, man. Here in chilly Minnesota, our mellow has been effectively harshed.

Looking back now, I wonder if their nonchalance was not about us at all, but was instead a general wariness toward the whole idea of marital commitment. Not that they don't believe in marriage. After all, they had been married for over thirty years themselves at that point. I think perhaps they just knew things about tying two lives together that we did not. Like the fact that a lot of the time it sucks.

CHAPTER 7

you're not doing it right

We're at Kennedy International Airport, newly married, heading off to a weeklong honeymoon. When debating where we should go, we came up with a bunch of ideas including Paris, Florence, the Caribbean, Barcelona, Costa Rica, and Thailand. Amsterdam did not make the list, but that is where we are going. One does not necessarily associate Amsterdam with "honeymoon destination." I don't know why, perhaps because of all the whores. But we go there because Amsterdam is the cheapest option and I have just paid for the entire wedding myself.

I don't really mind. The idea of the bride's parents paying for the wedding always seemed kind of antiquated to me anyway, although it would be great if she at least had a small dowry. Like maybe some goats or something.

I make myself feel better about spending all that money by thinking of the wedding as an investment in our future. Plus, if I amortize the costs of the wedding on an annual basis, the longer we stay married the less the wedding will have cost. For example, if we stay married for thirty thousand years, it works out to only a dollar a year.

Amsterdam became the most cost-effective place to vacation after we joined a home exchange program. This is a service that allows you to swap houses with people from all over the world. You just pick a place you want to go, work out compatible dates, and voila! Free lodging. We contacted people in all of the cities I just listed but could not find anybody who wanted to come to New York on the dates we were available. Our only offer came from a couple in Amsterdam, and we took it.

So now we're at the airport waiting on line at the ticket counter. Both of us are dreading the flight because it's an overnighter and we're stuck in coach since business and first-class tickets were outrageously expensive. But we'll try to sleep a little and hopefully it won't be too uncomfortable. Plus we're in love! (I cannot even persuade myself that love helps in coach.)

When we reach the counter, we present our passports and the agent says, "Are you newlyweds?"

"Yes," I say. "How did you know?"

"Your rings. They look brand-new."

Indeed they do—as bright and gleaming as our new marriage. Martha tells her we're going on our honeymoon.

The ticket agent smiles, taps some buttons on her keyboard, and hands us our tickets. It takes a second before we realize she's just upgraded us to first class. We thank her profusely. "Congratulations," she says. Marriage just became totally worth it.

Neither of us has ever flown in anything but steerage before so we're both excited to see the difference. When they

call for first-class passengers, we practically trip over ourselves to board the behemoth 747. The flight attendant looks
at our tickets and points us toward a shiny spiral staircase. I
have often wondered what is on the second floor of those big
airplanes. Now I know: heaven.

It's like a private lounge up there, dimly lit, spacious, fantastic. Instead of being crammed into five tiny seats abreast,
we each have our own private cocoon. The seats are enormous leather recliners outfitted with personal movie screens.
As soon as we sit down, our flight attendant gives us both
a little bag stuffed with toiletries, eye screens, and slippers.
Slippers! I put mine on immediately. Flying first class is great.
Flying first class while wearing slippers? Fucking amazing.
For the next several hours, they stuff us with food and drink
and toward the end of the flight, present us each with a little
earthenware Dutch house filled with liqueur. Slippers, food,
and adorable alcoholic collectibles?! WOW!

We land around dawn and attempt to give the taxi driver
our address, but the Dutch have inconsiderately written everything in their native language, making it very difficult for
visiting Americans like us to pronounce anything. The driver
seems unsure about where to go, so after driving around the
city for about exactly as long as he can before we start asking
him if he's ripping us off, the drab apartment building where
we are staying appears on some random street, a street whose
name I think translates to "some random street."

Mitigating the somewhat disappointing exterior, however,
are two factors. The first is that there are lots of cute bicycles
everywhere, making everything look cheerier. The second is

that our hosts are likely to be even more disappointed with our building in New York than I am with theirs. Because our place in New York is a shithole.

Inside, their apartment is spacious and attractively decorated. There's a big kitchen, living room, and a single large bedroom. Everything has that slightly off-kilter European look where it's all familiar-looking but at the same time kind of off. Not unpleasant but different. Pineapple juice in a box, for example. The whole place is like that.

After we unpack, the first thing I do is look through our host's photo albums because I am hoping there will be something naughty in there. I am in luck. There are several topless pictures of our hostess. She is young and fairly attractive and has good breasts. Because I am in Europe I do not think it inappropriate to stare at them for several minutes, nor do I consider it inappropriate to then go back and view them again repeatedly over the course of our trip. What *would* be inappropriate would be to masturbate to them.

We try to nap a little because we're jet-lagged but we are unable to sleep more than a couple of hours. Eventually we give up and try to figure out what to do with ourselves, which is when we run into our first problem.

Martha is the kind of traveler who likes to research her destination, find the best places to go, the finest restaurants in which to dine, and then plan a meticulous itinerary. I am the kind of traveler who likes to sit inside and watch TV. This naturally causes conflict when she wants to visit various Gothic cathedrals and I want to see what *Wheel of Fortune* sounds like in Dutch.

She tries to motivate me to do stuff with cheerful exhortations of "This is our honeymoon! We're supposed to do shit!"

I know, I know. Of course she is right. I am a terrible traveler. In later years, this will change as I begin to recognize that part of what makes travel fun and worthwhile is actually seeing the place you are paying to visit. At the moment, though, I am of the opinion that simply arriving at a destination is accomplishment enough.

Finally, I agree to take a walk with her around the neighborhood. Despite its debauched reputation, Amsterdam is a lovely city built on a series of concentric canals. These canals were conceived and created in the seventeenth century. I have no idea how the Dutch built citywide canals four hundred years ago without the benefit of either electricity or slaves, but somehow they did. Possibly they are a magic people. The Dutch also earn points in my book for hiding Jews during World War II, the most famous of whom was Anne Frank. Although I guess one could argue that they didn't do such a great job with her considering how that turned out.

We find an outdoor bazaar just down the street. It's a lot like the street fairs they have in New York, which is to say it's mostly just a bunch of vendors selling junk and socks. The main difference is that I cannot figure out how much anything costs and wind up buying a cheese sandwich for either two dollars or two hundred dollars.

We spend much of the day walking the cobblestone streets, darting in and out of unfailingly cute shops, and trying our best not to look overly American. Martha instructs me this means not yelling "Speak-ee English?" every time I need to talk to somebody.

Food-wise Amsterdam is pretty much crap, although we do discover *pannekoeken,* Dutch pancakes. There's a basement restaurant near us that serves them, and they are fantastic. *Pannekoeken* are thicker than a crepe, but thinner than American pancakes, and served either sweet or savory. Martha orders hers with ham and cheese. I get banana and Nutella. Although they are each big enough for two meals, we both clean our plates and promise to return.

That night we take a stroll through the famous red-light district. This is where the city's sex trade is plied. Prostitution is legal here, and the various painted ladies set up shop in small storefront windows, above each of which is a red light. Most of the women wear corny lingerie and pass the time sitting on stools smoking cigarettes. They pretty much all look bored or stoned. When a customer enters, the ladies pull a curtain closed and conduct their business. None of them makes much of an effort to attract the shifty-looking men wandering around other than the occasional halfhearted gyration vaguely directed toward the outside world. It is about as sexy as a trip to the DMV.

I have never been with a prostitute and do not think I ever could. Not because I have a particular moral objection to it since I feel like people should be free to do with their bodies what they want, but I just can't get into the idea of paying for sex. Does it impugn my masculinity to say that I don't crave sex enough to ever pay for a blowjob? Maybe. But it's true; what's also true is that I am uncomfortably like the stereotypical female who needs emotional stimulation as much as physical. If I don't believe that my partner is as invested in the sucking and fucking as I am, then I can't get into it, either. Guys aren't supposed to care about stuff like that, but I do. So much so that I don't think I could even get an erection with a hooker. Then I would feel bad about it because I would be afraid her feelings would be hurt, and then I would start overapologizing, which would just make everything worse. So I think it's better if I just stay away from such things. Plus, I guess there's the fact that I'm married.

Also scattered around the red-light district are clusters of "coffee shops." In Amsterdam, this means "marijuana store." I don't know why they don't just call them that, but they don't. They're all pretty much identical: a few couches, some Bob Marley posters on the walls, dreadlocked twenty-somethings at the counter, the burbling sound of hookahs. Occasionally we see some passed-out dude on the floor, presumably American, and I think to myself, *What an idiot.*

My experience with marijuana is limited. I have none. Again, this is not because I have a moral objection to its use, but because I am afraid to smoke anything. I don't like the idea of inhaling anything into my lungs, and so I have never tried cigarettes or pot. But I am in Amsterdam and resolve that while here I will give it a go.

A few nights later, after a long day of sightseeing followed by a big Italian meal, we choose a coffee shop at random. I am still nervous about smoking, so instead we order a huge "space cake," a dense brownie baked with pot. It tastes bad. Like equal parts chocolate and lawn clippings. I am stuffed from the meal we've just eaten, but I force down the chalky dessert and wait for delirium.

Nothing happens.

"Are you feeling anything?" I keep asking Martha.

"Not yet."

"Because I'm not feeling anything," I say. "But I don't know what I'm supposed to feel and I'm afraid I'm going to miss it."

"Be patient," she says.

I try to be patient but I grow increasingly convinced it's not working. Maybe we didn't eat enough space cake. Or all the pasta in my stomach soaked up the THC.

Martha's eyes go to half-mast. "I'm starting to feel it," she says.

"I'm not feeling anything," I say. Forty-five minutes have elapsed and I feel exactly the same.

"Be patient," she counsels again.

I wait another five minutes or so. Her head is bopping along to the Bob Marley. She seems mildly dazed and I am jealous.

"Let's get a joint," I say, thinking that maybe I need to bypass my stomach and infuse my bloodstream through my lungs. If I'm going to get high, maybe I just need to conquer my fears and smoke.

"Are you sure?" she asks.

"Yeah."

"I don't think you've waited long enough."

"It's been, like, an hour."

"Okay."

"You get it," I tell her.

"Why me?"

"Because I feel stupid."

"Fine," she says and goes to the counter. She orders something mild from them and returns to the table with a good-size blunt.

"Show me how to smoke it."

She lights it, and explains how you suck the smoke down into your lungs, hold it, and release. I copy her actions but nothing comes out of my mouth when I exhale. Then she says something for the first time in our marriage, five words that neatly sum up my own feelings about my entire life:

"You're not doing it right," she says.

I try again. And again. A few smoky wisps escape my nose and mouth, but whatever I'm doing isn't working. I don't feel anything. Meanwhile, Martha is slouched down in her chair with a goofy smile on her face. What am I doing wrong? I take another hit and another.

"It's not working," I complain.

The joint is getting smaller between my fingers until it is almost gone. Suddenly I hear somebody screaming. It's a female voice, coming from close by, and the woman sounds terrified.

"Help!" the voice is screaming. "He's dying! He's dying!"

What's going on?

And then I realize: I am unconscious. The woman screaming is my wife.

I have now become that asshole American passed out on the floor of the coffee shop.

Then I feel a hand at the back of my head and a glass pushed toward my mouth. The unseen hand forces a sweet sugary liquid into my mouth. My eyes open. Martha is staring at me, panic-stricken. One of the dreadlocked guys is beside me, his hand on my shoulder, holding me upright.

"Are you okay?" she asks me. I do not answer because I no longer have a mouth. She turns to the guy. "I think he's dying!" she yells.

"Nobody ever died from pot," he drawls. Then he disappears in a puff of smoke.

Martha is wild-eyed. "Are you okay?"

I nod but no words come out. My head feels thick and mushy, like a bowl of oatmeal. I watch her lips move.

"You passed out. You were yelling at me that it wasn't working and then your head hit the table and you fell off your chair and landed on the floor."

I nod again. Her lips remind me of kite strings and I find myself thinking about panda bears. Panda bears do not fly kites, I tell myself.

"I thought you were dead," she says.

Maybe if you taped a kite to a panda paw and scared the panda so that it started running, the kite might start to lift off. I clench and unclench my fist to make sure I still have motor control. I seem to, although I am concerned that if I touch anything my hand may pass right through it since we are all made from atoms and atoms are mostly empty space.

"Are you okay?" she asks again and again. I nod again and again. I do not know if I am okay. I do not know if I even exist at this point. I make a motorboat noise and sip some more sugar water. I'm high. She's high, too, and freaking out. "Should we leave?" she asks. I nod.

We stand up and help each other outside. The air is cool. It feels good. All these atoms pressed against me. Mmmm.

"I forgot my purse," she says. "Stay here."

I sit on the curb, pushing down against the cobblestones with my feet so that they do not float up above my head and pull me upside down into the sky. I sit like this and watch the night carnival pass by, all the horny young men and middle-aged tourists and locals heading home from pubs and I see myself in their eyes and am appalled.

"I'm not American!" I yell at them because I love my country and do not want them thinking ill of us.

The walk back to the apartment is long and confusing, particularly because, after thinking about panda bears, I discover that I have now *become* a panda bear, and must walk like a panda bear through the streets.

"Why are you walking like that?" she asks.

I try to tell her about the pandas flying their kites, but she does not understand. What's not to understand?

Then we are in bed and this logy feeling will not go away and I tell her I cannot sleep like this how much longer will it last just a couple more hours she says but I don't know because I think the air pressure is different than it used to be and that can't be good and maybe it's not the drugs that make me feel like this but maybe we are now living in an entirely different atmosphere and eventually I pass out and when it is morning I open my eyes and the sun is out and I am just as high as when I went to bed and I want to cry.

"This is never going to end!" I yell.

Martha seems to feel a little better. She helps me out of

bed and pushes me to the bathroom. I take a shower, hoping a hard blast of water will jolt me back into my body, but it is a European shower, so the pressure is not sufficient to do anything more than smear me with water. The plumbing in Europe is terrible. Also, I will never get used to the idea of "shower gel" no matter how many times I use it.

Amsterdam breakfasts are better than the ones at home, which are always too heavy for my taste. Here in Holland we eat cold cuts and hard-boiled eggs and a slice of bread with butter and (my favorite part) chocolate sprinkles. The food tastes great this morning.

"We should eat more chocolate sprinkles for breakfast when we get home," I tell Martha.

She sips her coffee and says nothing. I interpret this as agreement and resolve to buy sprinkles first thing when we return. I will say this for being high: it makes chocolate sprinkles taste *amazing*.

I am better by the middle of the day, but I do not feel like doing much. Martha takes a walk and I masturbate to topless pictures of our hostess.

The night before we leave, we polish our wedding bands so they look as shiny as possible. On line at the airport we try to look lovey-dovey, but I tell her maybe we should tone it down because customs might think we're high and search our bags. When we reach the counter, we make sure to flash our rings and casually mention to the ticket agent that we're newlyweds. She does not seem to care.

"We're just getting back from our honeymoon," I say.

The ticket agent looks up from her computer and warmly

says, "Congratulations," then taps at her keyboard. I shoot Martha a hopeful look. The agent gives us a big smile as she hands us our tickets.

No upgrade. Shit.

The airplane seats in coach are even tinier than I expected, probably a result of the roomy splendor we reveled in on the trip over. Perhaps the first-class trip wasn't worth it because it is going to make our trip home so much worse by comparison. I give Martha the window seat and take the middle one for myself because I am a saint. A large teenage girl sits next to me. Soon we are surrounded by large teenage girls. They are seriously the largest teenage girls I have ever seen.

It turns out the girls are a Russian basketball team and they are loud. Within an hour they are also drunk. I know it's a cliché to say that Russians drink a lot of vodka, but sometimes clichés are the God's honest truth. These girls drink from wheels up to wheels down and do not stop their annoying, guttural Slavic chatter even for a second. The Russians have a word to describe situations like this. So do the Americans. That word is *horrible*.

More to herself than to me, Martha says, "I don't think I can do this." I don't think I can do it either. But we do it.

Arriving back in New York, we are just another haggard married couple dragging our baggage home. Yes, there are wedding presents waiting for us back at our apartment, which will be fun to open and return, but now we've got to figure out what it means to be married. Hopefully, it doesn't mean making a baby anytime soon.

CHAPTER 8

terrified because it's terrifying

Martha wants a baby. We've been married for a couple of years and now she wants a kid. We have discussed having children before and each agree that we want them, but we have some disagreements about quantity and timing. She is thinking three. I am thinking one. She is thinking now. I am thinking not now.

"When?" she asks.

"Not now," I answer. There is no other answer. There is now and there is not now. The appropriate time to have children is not now.

"But it's a perfect time. I'm not working," she says.

It's true. She is not working. But the reason she is not working is that she is not looking for work. If she actually looked for a job, she might find one, which would make it an imperfect time to have a baby.

"I don't want to be an old mom," she says. "Let's just get it over with."

The statement "let's just get it over with" does not give me a lot of confidence in Martha's preparedness for motherhood. Then again, she has a point. If we start having kids now, we'll still be relatively young when they move out of the house. Is that a reason to start having children? Should I begin the most important undertaking of my life by rationalizing that the sooner I start, the sooner I will be done?

I guess so.

Here's the thing: Neither Martha nor I *love* kids. We're not like some people we know who pine for children. The stuff that I pine for usually either tastes delicious or requires AAA batteries. Yes, I want kids, but I want them in an abstract way, the way I want, say, a jukebox. Once in a while I think to myself how fun it would be to have a jukebox. *It sure would be neat to have a jukebox,* I might think to myself. But I am not actually going to buy one. Because they are big and expensive and because that would be stupid.

There are no such obstacles preventing me from having a kid. Kids are small and can live in one of our rooms. The cost of manufacture is minimal. Making babies is free. Or almost free—you do have to get the lady drunk first. Maybe there *should* be a fee for making babies; there would probably be a lot fewer of them running around if there were. (Actually, that's a pretty good idea: charge people for sex, although now that I think about it, I realize that idea has already been tried—quite successfully.)

After many discussions about the matter, and faced with a depleting store of excuses as to why this is not a good time, I agree to start making babies. And so begins the first truly purposeful fucking of my life.

Trying to make a baby is like getting a job as a roller-coaster inspector. When you first get the job, you're like, "Oh boy, I get to ride roller coasters every day for my job!" But by the end of the third or fourth day, it's not nearly as much fun riding roller coasters, and after a month or two you are probably pretty sick of roller coasters altogether. And so it is with making a baby. The two most dreaded words I hear every month are "I'm ovulating." Soon the act of copulating becomes as ritualized and dull as milking a cow. I am the cow.

Moo.

After a few weeks, Martha brings home a small plastic bag from the pharmacy. Inside is a cardboard box containing detailed instructions about how she is supposed to pee on the enclosed stick. She follows the instructions and we wait for the magic stick to divine our future. Negative.

Three months elapse. Four months. Five.

As the six-month mark approaches, the inevitable questions start to arise in each of our minds. Is something wrong with one of us? We tell each other it is early yet, not to worry, no problem. But I do not fully believe my reassurances to her, and I do not think she believes hers to me. Each of us thinks something might be wrong, and each of us blames the other. Because that's the kind of people we are.

Outwardly, I am willing to at least entertain the notion that our inability to get pregnant is *my* fault, but the actual fact of the matter is that I know it is not. I know this with a high degree of certainty. But I cannot tell her how I know this because the reason is too embarrassing.

This is how I know:

When I was a sophomore in college, I applied to be a sperm donor. Like many decisions I have made in my life this one was not well thought-out. I saw an ad in the college newspaper looking for sperm donors, calculated how much money I could get by doing something I did already for free, and decided to apply.

I briefly considered the ethical ramifications of donating sperm. How would I feel about the potential of creating new people I would never know or even know about? How would I feel about my genetic material getting mixed up with random eggs in random places? Might I spend the rest of my life eyeing every gorgeous young person who came across my path and wonder, *Did I make that?*

Was that kind of lifelong uncertainty worth fifty dollars a pop? Yes. If it meant I didn't have to get a job delivering pizzas, yes. (I later got a job delivering pizzas. Jerking off is a better job.)

The clinic is a low-slung, impersonal building nestled into an anonymous strip of dingy stores. Hardware store, deli, sperm donation center. The closer I get, the more apprehensive I begin to feel. Maybe this was a bad idea. Maybe somebody I know will see me go in. Worse, maybe somebody I know will be in the waiting room. Or what if I find myself waiting for my turn outside the room used to conduct your business, and the person who comes out is my roommate, Richard? That would really be awkward. Especially if he is still holding his sample.

I consider turning around and going back to my dorm. Except that I really could use the money. Even if I just donate twice a month, that would be an extra hundred dollars in my pocket, a lot of money for me in those days. It is admittedly not very much money on a per-sperm basis, but still.

To forestall my decision, I decide to go to the deli next door for a sandwich, and then assess how I feel. I cross the street and make for the deli. Just as I am about to enter, however, I detour into the clinic. (I am extremely gullible when I lie to myself.)

Inside, the clinic is small and unassuming. It looks like the waiting room for a mediocre accountant. I am the only one there. I approach the receptionist and mumble to her that I would like to apply to become a donor. She is a bit older than me and faceless. Or maybe she has a face but I cannot see it because I cannot look her in the eye. She shoves a clipboard at me and tells me to fill out the attached paperwork, informing me as I do that they only accept a small number of applicants because they are seeking people with "unusually high sperm count and motility." I'm not sure what motility is, so I look it up later. It means how much they wiggle. Wigglier sperm are better.

After I'm finished with the paperwork, a nurse leads me to a tiny, antiseptic, fluorescent-lit room. This is the Masturbation Chamber. Until I visit an actual sadomasochistic dungeon a couple of years later, it is the oddest place for sexual activity I have ever encountered. It looks like the kind of room where you might get fitted for orthopedic shoes, except that there is also a leather recliner and a cheap coffee table fanned with a vast assortment of pornographic magazines should I require "assistance." I do not know where to put my eyes as the receptionist hands me a plastic Dixie cup in which to "deposit my specimen." I take the cup. She instructs me to leave my specimen behind a little metal door built into the wall. Then she leaves and I am left to contemplate whether I can complete my assigned task.

No. No, there's no way. First of all, there's no way any part of my body is going to touch that recliner. Nor am I going to page through any of those well-thumbed magazines, not unless they are first laminated and then sprayed down with industrial bleach. Also, I just do not think I am physically capable of getting it up in this environment. I should go back out there and return my empty cup to the receptionist because this is not going to be possible.

I'm done in about ninety seconds. In fact, I do it so fast that I'm actually kind of embarrassed, so I wait around in the room for an additional couple of minutes until it seems like a less freakishly short amount of time has elapsed. Once I decide enough time has passed for a man to complete his ejaculatory business, I leave my no-longer-empty Dixie cup in its appointed place and flee the building, mortified. In a weird way, my emotional reaction to masturbating into a cup is not so different from my emotional reaction to much of my youthful lovemaking with actual girls: both experiences end with a fair amount of shame and regret.

A few weeks later, I receive a call in my dorm room telling me the lab results are back: my sperm are unspectacular. Normal, yes, but unimpressive both in terms of quantity and dance skills. Therefore, I am not an acceptable candidate for donation. I am both relieved and insulted. My sperm are not good enough to be turkey-basted into the wombs of random ladies? How dare they!

Since that time I have not been exposed to any serious

amounts of radiation, so years later, when I approach the act of marital copulation, I am secure in the knowledge that my swimmers may not be distinguished but they are functional. They are, now that I think about it, a lot like me.

Martha does not know about this incident in my past (until now) and so when we are slow to conceive I go along with the charade that, if there is a problem, it might reside with me. Even so, I keep reassuring her that we're probably fine. All the books (and she has begun amassing many books on the subject) say it's not unusual for conception to take a year or so. We've barely been at it six months, so we're only halfway up the "legitimate cause for alarm" growth chart.

Every month that goes by with a wasted pee stick finds a small part of me secretly relieved. Maybe even a medium-size part. If we can't have a baby, I won't have to be a father. Which might be okay with me, because I don't think I will be very good at it. My own dad wasn't, and I have no reason to think I'll be any better. I'm not even sure what a father is supposed to do other than complain about having to shave. Other things I know dads do: drink coffee, worry about the price of things, and tell their kids to go pick rocks out of the lawn.

Is there some sort of paternal instinct that kicks in when a baby is born? Or is it supposed to already be here? Because if it's already supposed to be here, I'm screwed. What if my sperm turn out to be fine but my dad gene lacks motility? Is there a stick I can pee on to determine what kind of father I will be?

My biggest fear is that I will be a bad father. Maybe I will be the sort of father who only knows how to express himself with rage. Perhaps I will be the sort of abusive father who makes his kid turn to drugs. How many books have been written about terrible fathers? I do not want to be the sort of father that inspires art.

So when Martha does not become pregnant right away I feel relief. Maybe we are not destined for parenthood. Perhaps we will end up one of those sad childless couples who spend all their time sleeping late, buying luxury goods, traveling the world, and enjoying each other's company. That would be terrible.

Or what if she wants to adopt? That would be a good thing to do, I guess, but where would we get the kid? The Eastern Bloc countries are out: all their babies come with weird abnormalities like flipper hands. China is too trendy. We could maybe get an American baby, but chances are it would end up being a black baby and that just seems like we're trying too hard, like, "Look at us and our black baby." Maybe Guatemala?

On the sixth month, I am in the bedroom waiting for Martha to come out of the bathroom with her negative pregnancy stick. But when the door to the bathroom opens, she is, instead, with child.

"I'm pregnant," she says.

She holds the test up for me to see—two little lines etched in blue.

Oh wow. Wow. I go to her. We hug and kiss. I put my hand on her stomach.

"Wow," I say.

"Are you happy?" she asks.

"Yes. Are you?"

"Yes."

I'm not sure I believe either of us. Am I happy? I am. At least a certain, small percentage of my prefrontal cortex is pinging something I recognize as happiness. How much? Twenty-three percent. Another 19 percent feels relief at having accomplished the task of impregnating my wife. The rest, the other 58 percent of my emotional state, can be described as terrified—because it is terrifying.

We confirm her pregnancy with another home test, followed by a trip to Martha's gynecologist. They all say the same thing. Baby.

"Congratulations," the doctor says, the first person to congratulate us. We thank her and smile and think our private thoughts. Baby.

All thoughts now end in the word *baby*. Everything we say or do, every action, every mile we drive, the food we eat, the books we read, the shows we watch. All colors. All smells. Baby.

We agree to keep the news secret for the first few weeks. No use alerting our friends and relatives until we discern whether the pregnancy is "viable," a term I have always found a touch unsettling because it makes it sound as if we've done something scientifically unproven, like crossbred a human with a walrus.

Although Martha has sworn me to secrecy, she immediately tells everybody she knows. Our friends Kerri and Lora, her friends Romy and Kaela, her hairstylist, bus drivers, homeless people. Sometimes she just calls random people from the phone book to tell them. When I finally start informing my friends a month or so later that Martha is pregnant, pretty much everybody I tell says, "I know."

I'm careful never to use the expression *"we're* pregnant," because I hate it. We are not pregnant. Martha is. No matter how many times I pee on a stick, I remain decidedly not pregnant. When I hear couples say "we're pregnant," it always makes me think they are starring in a terrible Hollywood comedy in which, because of some zany scientific mishap, both partners in a relationship end up carrying a baby. In the trailer they're having an adorable argument standing in their impossibly well-decorated home and we hear a drip, drip, drip sound. The guy and the girl (played by Ashton Kutcher and Reese Witherspoon respectively) look down and each say at the same time, "I think your water just broke."

Pregnancy does not agree with Martha. She feels sick right away. The worst of it is nausea, which begins every morning and stays with her in varying degrees throughout the day. Her sense of smell intensifies, and everything she smells just makes her feel sicker. Her appetite slackens. She loses weight. She's depressed. On top of that, we've recently bought our first house, a century-old Dutch Colonial, which needs a lot of work. Also, we have a new puppy. And, on top of everything else, I am acting like a total cock.

I wish it weren't so, but it's true. I am surly and terse and completely unsympathetic to her condition. You feel sick?

It's your fault for making a baby. You feel tired? Sucks for you, lady. You want the baby's room painted? Here's a step-ladder.

One would think a good partner would not make his pregnant wife climb up and down stepladders all day inhaling paint fumes in order to paint a baby nursery. And one would be correct to think that about a good partner. But I am not being a good partner. I am the guy saying, "Hey, the room looks fine to me. If you want it painted, paint it yourself."

So she does. She spends several days painting the baby's room by herself, while I stew in my office. I define "stewing" as playing online poker for ten hours at a time.

Why am I being such a total prick?

The only excuse I have is fear masquerading as denial manifesting itself as assholishness. If we don't paint the baby's room, maybe we won't have a baby, and if we don't have a baby, maybe I won't fail at being a father.

I blame Martha for my fear. *She* is the one who wanted this baby. *She* forced us to make this child. Why did it have to be now? Why couldn't we wait a little longer? Why does everything have to be on her schedule? I feel unprepared and scared and rather than deal with my feelings I just push her awayawayaway. Maybe if I push hard enough she really will go away.

"Yes, I know the smell of tuna makes you throw up, Martha. Does that mean I no longer have the right to eat tuna from a can? Are you going to take THAT away from me too, just like YOU TOOK AWAY MY FREEDOM?"

It never occurs to me to ask if she is scared, too.

About six weeks in, we're in a dim examination room at the ob-gyn's office. Her doctor is a middle-aged Pakistani woman who seems very capable. I base my assessment of her competence on the expert way she squeezes ultrasound goop from a ketchup bottle onto Martha's belly.

"This will be a little cold," she says. And it is cold. She's a very good doctor.

The doctor picks up a flat white paddle and runs it over the goop. A maze of shadowy images flicker onto the ultrasound monitor beside us. We're peeking inside Martha's belly. It's amazing and weird and kind of gross.

"There," the doctor says.

On the screen is a kidney-shaped object the size of a grain of rice. It's our baby. We can see something moving within. The heart, a tiny flickering strobe light.

"Do you want to hear?" she asks.

I didn't know this thing has audio. Yes, of course we want to hear. She pushes a button on the machine and a wet whooshing pulse fills the room. *Hwaah hwaah hwaah hwaah.* Oh wow. It sounds like an underwater dance club in there.

Why is its heart beating so fast? That's normal. How does everything else look? Normal. Everything's normal? Yes. Are you sure? Yes. We stare, mesmerized. That's our kid in there. Or a tadpole. It's still too soon to tell which one. But one thing is definite. In a matter of months, we will either be the proud parents of a baby or a frog. The doctor prints out a photo of our blob to take home. It doesn't look like much, but we tack it to the refrigerator when we get home.

In preparation for the baby's arrival, I decide I need a new desk. No doubt this is due to a natural biological impulse common among expectant parents to start nesting. Why I feel the baby needs a giant old-fashioned government surplus steel desk for my home office is unclear, but that's what my nesting instinct tells me to go out and purchase.

Our new house is in Peekskill, New York, one of those always-dying, never-quite-dead Hudson River communities that used to manufacture things back when America did that. We bought our home there because it is the only community within an hour of New York City that we can afford. Among its many shortcomings is the fact that there are no stores in Peekskill that sell old-fashioned government surplus steel desks. I make some calls around the area and finally find a place that does in Poughkeepsie, about an hour north.

Driving up there in my silver Volkswagen New Beetle (not a girl's car), I lose the signals from my usual New York radio stations and have to scan around for another choice, finally settling on a random rock station called the Fox or the Cat or the Cobra or some other animal I do not associate with rock and roll. As I pull into Poughkeepsie, they play a song I have never heard before by a band I only know from their one previous hit, a band pretty much universally acknowledged to be shitty: Creed.

I am not a music snob. If anything, my musical taste is bad by any critical standards. My favorite song of all time is "Come On Eileen" by Dexys Midnight Runners. A close second is "MMMBop" by Hanson. So I am not out there claiming any musical superiority, but Creed really does suck. Bad music, pretentious lyrics, and a messianic front man. Also they are from Florida. No good rock music has ever come from Florida. Undoubtedly, there will be legions of offended Floridian readers who think to themselves, *What are you talking about? Such-and-such band is from Florida and they're freaking awesome!* No. Whatever band you are thinking of, if they are from Florida, they suck. Not as much as Creed, but they still suck.

So I am driving through downtown Poughkeepsie when this song by Floridian cock-rockers Creed comes on the radio. The song is called "With Arms Wide Open." It opens with these lyrics:

Well, I just heard the news today
It seems my life is going to change

I cannot reprint any more of the lyrics here because I asked Creed's permission to do so, but they refused my request. I'm not sure why, but I suspect it had something to do with saying how much they suck in the above paragraphs.

To summarize, the song goes on to describe the narrator's reaction to finding out he is going to be a father, a reaction infinitely more mature than my own. For one thing, he is going to greet the baby, per the title, with arms wide open, whereas I seem to be welcoming my own baby with arms resolutely folded across my chest. The song then discusses the "awe" the singer feels, his gratitude, and his fervent wish that the child grow up to be a better man than he himself is. I don't know what kind of man Scott Stapp is, but I certainly hope his unborn child is a better singer.

I am wholly unprepared for my reaction to this song, which is uncontrollable, sustained, violent weeping. Within seconds of registering the song's subject matter, I am crying so hard I feel like I've just been punched in the tear ducts with a raw onion. The tears seem to come from a deep liquid reservoir somewhere near my solar plexus, some gland I did not know about that stores salt water by the gallon. All of this smirking detachment in which I have encased myself over the past few months is no match for the awesome power of Creed.

I am crying so hard I have to pull my masculine automobile over to the side of the road so that I can sob without danger of driving into a tree. Thank God Poughkeepsie is in even worse financial condition than Peekskill; there is nobody on the sidewalks to see me hunched over in my front seat, arms crossed at midsection, holding myself into a solid shape so that I do not leak out of the car in a quivering protoplasmic goo. For long minutes, well after lead singer Scott Stapp has finished singing his stupid, pompous, corny-ass song that I love more than any song I have ever heard before, I sit in my car and cry.

I am undone.

At the time, I think these tears are nothing, a hormonal hiccup, a perfectly normal stress reaction. But now, years later, now that my son is ten, now that I have a daughter who is eight, now that I know fatherhood for what it is, I think that incident stemmed from something else. Or, actually, two things.

The first is a deep recognition of time, the long stretches of time that have brought me here to Poughkeepsie, coupled with an unfolding future that extends to some distant dim place where my children will live, our children's children will live, and on and on. And here I am parked outside a surplus office furniture store, one moment in a long series of moments.

The second is recognizing that these tears are nostalgia in its deepest sense, the sharp pain of remembering and the equally sharp pain of hope. There is no word for feeling nostalgic about the future, but that's what a parent's tears often are, a nostalgia for something that has not yet occurred. They are the pain of hope, the helplessness of hope, and finally, the surrender to hope. That's what parenthood is, ultimately, the hope of casting a message in a glass bottle into the sea with no sense of where it will end up. We have no control, none of us.

Creed changed my life.

After ten minutes or so, I pull myself together and go into the store to make my purchase. I drag the battered old desk out to the car and contemplate how I am going to fit this thing into my Beetle. It is a battleship, far bigger than I expected. Too big for me to know how to deal with it. But here it is. But it's what I wanted, and here it is. For half an hour, I struggle with the desk, lifting it a bit at a time. One corner, then another. First inside the car, then out. I wrestle with it and tear at it and unscrew the feet, and then the legs, and eventually I get the thing tamed. I secure it as best as I can with some old rope and start the long trip back to Peekskill, this monstrous weight threatening to tip me over. I drive in silence, radio off. I drive slow. We are pregnant and I have to get home.

Baby.

CHAPTER 9

dead dad kid

My own father seemed to know so much. He could operate a ham radio. He knew how to make corned beef hash. My brother and he once turned an ordinary block of wood into an excellent soapbox derby car. He was also very good at painting tiny lead figurines of wizards. From a kid's point of view, it was a pretty impressive knowledge base.

But he wasn't the best father. Not because he didn't love us, but because he simply didn't know how to be around kids. He wasn't socially adept with adults, either, but with children he was hopeless. He didn't wrestle or make dumb faces or play catch. A popular activity when we visited my dad on the weekends? He would hand my brother and me each a plastic bucket and tell us to go outside and pick the rocks out of his lawn. Once, he bought me a baseball mitt for my birthday, which I loved except for the fact that I am a lefty and he bought me a right-handed mitt. It seemed equally possible to me that he was either unaware that baseball mitts came for both righties and lefties, or that he did not know I am left-handed.

Here is how he died: one night, the police find him pulled over in his car on the side of the highway. He's unconscious with a head injury, the apparent victim of an assault. They think it occurred in the parking lot at Rutgers University, where he is taking night classes to get his master's degree. He is thirty-nine years old.

He is brought to the hospital, where doctors perform emergency brain surgery. My brother, Eric, and I aren't told until the following day, after he is out of immediate danger. I don't remember who took us to visit him a couple of days later: Mom or his second wife, Beth. My parents have been divorced for seven years, and their relationship is terrible. So it was probably Beth.

I *do* remember how frail Dad looks. His head is shaved and a long crescent-shape scar circumnavigates his skull. He seems distant and foggy, and we don't stay long.

A few weeks later, he is out of the hospital and home for the holidays. Beth gives him teddy bears that Christmas. Lots of teddy bears, including a baseball cap with a teddy bear sewn onto the brim. The cap covers the scar, although I would have a hard time determining which looks worse, the scar or the hat.

Over the next few months, his recovery is slower than expected but he does not seem to be in any danger. Then one morning, we're asleep in our bunk beds. It's early, a school day. I hear Mom come into the room. "Boys, wake up," she says. My eyes open. She's standing beside our bunk bed where she can see us both. She is unhesitant: "Your father died last night."

She says it quick, almost blowing the words out with her breath. He was readmitted to the hospital . . . an infection in his leg . . . they gave him a medicine he was allergic to . . . it said so on his chart . . . an accident . . . "I'm so sorry," she says, and I can see her struggling to retain her composure for us, but she can't hold herself together. She begins weeping huge, convulsive sobs, then collapses onto the floor, falling to her knees so that her face is level with mine in the bottom bunk. She is crying so hard she is struggling to breathe. I have never seen her like this. "I'm so sorry," she says again and again. She runs from the room, leaving Eric and me alone.

The news is so swift and shocking that I cannot process it at all. Above me, I hear Eric begin to cry, and after a moment, I start crying, too, because I don't know what else to do. Crying seems like the appropriate response and I am still young enough, twelve, that I can summon tears without too much effort. As we lie in bed, I wonder if I will have to go to school today. No, no school today or for the rest of the week. When Mom calls to tell them I won't be coming in for a while, I ask if she can tell them it's because I'm sick, and not because my dad died. "Can you tell them I have tonsillitis?" I ask. Mom gives me a strange, perplexed look, like I just levitated. She doesn't understand why I wouldn't want to tell people the truth. She doesn't understand that dead dads are embarrassing; they attract unwanted attention. When I return to school, I am afraid people will stare at me and point: "There goes the kid with the dead dad. Hey, Dead Dad Kid!"

People make fun of me enough already because I am younger than everybody else in my class, and because all my close friends are girls, and because I once gave a speech for sixth-grade class president wearing a rubber Alfred E. Neuman Halloween mask. (I did not win.) For years afterward, people mockingly called me "Alfred."

So I don't really need any additional attention.

"What about appendicitis?" I ask. "Can we tell them I have appendicitis?"

"We'll tell them the truth," she says.

I hate the truth.

She takes Eric and me to work with her that day because there is nowhere else for us to go. She and Elaine own a small stationery store in an indoor flea market, selling personalized stationery, greeting cards, and novelty items like giant plastic Budweiser bottles that people use as savings banks. I hate working there.

The day passes in a haze. We don't talk about Dad. We don't talk about anything. Instead we perform our normal store functions. For Eric, that means being helpful. For me, that means stealing money out of the cash register. I routinely steal quarters from my mother's store to use at the arcade, which may at least partially explain why the store ultimately fails, and *definitely* explains why I ultimately become very good at the game *Time Pilot*.

On our way home from work, we stop at the video store. Mom tells us we can pick out whatever movie we want. We choose *The Blues Brothers,* which is rated R. Normally we are not allowed to rent R-rated movies, so I am a little nervous as we hand it to her. She glances at the box, but doesn't say anything. Awesome. A small, shameful part of me begins to see an upside to Dad dying. For the foreseeable future, it seems like I will get away with whatever I want: skipping school,

R-rated movies, maybe even the Holy Grail of childhood con-
traband, sugar cereals. Our cereal cupboard is normally filled
with high-fiber, lesbian-friendly cereals like Product 19 and
Special K. (Yes, there are lesbian-friendly breakfast cereals.)
Surely a boy who has just lost his father is not to be denied a
box or two of Frosted Flakes in his grief. Surely not.

Even as I am having these thoughts I am aware what a
horrible person I must be. Who thinks like this? Who thinks
about using the death of a parent as a means to get sugar? As
it turns out, me. I do that. Why do I not feel tormented with
grief? Isn't that what you're supposed to feel when a parent
dies? Am I defective? That first day, I honestly feel like getting to miss school and watch *The Blues Brothers* is a pretty fair
trade for losing my dad.

The next morning, Mom takes us suit shopping for the funeral. We go to a local store—Von Goodman's or something—
and when the salesman asks if we need help, Mom tells him
the whole story: dead father, funeral, suits. I am mortified. She
forces me to try to on several bunchy outfits before we (she)
finally settle on a somber navy blue jacket and pants, white
shirt, new black dress shoes, clip-on tie. Eric is dressed almost
identically. We look like a couple of junior Jehovah's Witnesses.

"You look stupid," I say.

"You look worse," he responds.

"You look like a retard."

"You look like a gay retard."

Touché.

We have nothing to do before the funeral two days from
now, so we sit around the basement by ourselves watching

game shows and soap operas. We don't talk about it. Anyway, what is there to say?

"It sucks that Dad died."

"Yeah."

"Can you turn *The Price Is Right* on?"

"Sure."

I keep flashing back to an incident that happened a year or so before, when Dad was dropping us off at home after one of our weekends with him. He was not a demonstrative man, and it occurred to me that I couldn't remember him ever telling me that he loved me. I didn't doubt that he did, but he'd never said it, and I had never said it to him. So I decided to tell him I loved him. I'm not sure why I felt the need to do it at that moment, but it seemed important.

I waited for Eric and Susan to get out of the car, and when they were clear, I gathered up my courage and blurted out, "I love you, Dad." Then I ran from the car, up the sidewalk, and into the house. If he responded, I never heard. That's what I keep thinking about in the basement as Rick and I watch *The Price Is Right* on TV, the big Showcase Showdown wheel spinning on its axis around and around and around.

I'm nervous about the funeral. I've never been to one and I don't know if I'm going to have to look at Dad's dead body or not. What if I don't want to? What if I cry a lot and everybody looks at me? Are people allowed to make fun of you at a funeral? Also, will there be food?

The next day, our stepmother, Beth, picks us up, and we drive with her to the funeral home, a saggy old Victorian house near the highway. Inside, the place suffocates from wood and carpet. A long hallway bisects the building leading to several viewing rooms, which, I think, is also what they call them in adult video stores. Beth asks if I want to go into the viewing room where they've got Dad.

"In a minute," I say, taking a seat on a bench in the hallway. She and Eric walk into the room together and I sit by myself. I do not want to go in—absolutely do not want to go. It's going to be creepy and I do not like creepy things. Even *Scooby-Doo* stresses me out.

There are a lot of people milling around I do not recognize. Work friends, maybe. People he knew from his neighborhood. My aunt Jane is also there with our cousins Michelle and Robyn. Our grandfather whom we rarely see is there. He doesn't say much. He doesn't cry, doesn't hug me or even shake my hand. All in all, he seems remarkably unperturbed. He lives another twenty years, but I never see him again.

Somebody checks on me. Am I okay? I nod. Yeah, yeah. Never better. My new suit is uncomfortable and itchy around the armpits. Also, I feel like I can't breathe. And I might throw up. I'm good.

When I crane my neck, I can see the edge of the coffin through the door frame. If I stay in the hallway, do I still get credit for having attended the funeral? Because I really don't want to go in. Eventually, I am the only one left out there.

Beth comes out and tells me they're about to start. If I'm going to go in, I should go in now. I do. I walk in, her hand on my shoulder guiding me forward. Eric is already seated in the front row. Ahead is the coffin and inside the open casket is my dad. I see him now and I want to turn back. We get right up to it and I stare at my father's face, the last time I will ever see it. He looks okay. He looks like himself. I guess I expected to see some elemental change in him, some subtle but definitive signifier that says, "This guy is dead." The fact that he's inside a coffin does a pretty good job of that, I guess, but I thought there would be something else, some sort of mark. But there's not. He just looks like Dad, and it feels wrong that he should look the same.

I'd heard people say the dead look like they're asleep, but that doesn't seem right to me. Sleeping people drool, and fidget, and fart. Dad looks like something other than asleep; he looks *arranged*. He looks like the idea of a person instead of a person, like the kind of thing God would have made in seventh-grade art class. I could reach out and touch him if I want to, but I don't. I just need to stare at him a little longer because I am never going to see him again and I try to sear his face into my memory. It doesn't work.

I have a hard time really remembering what he looked like that day. But I can remember the feeling of his hand on my head when I am six and we are at Indian Guides, and I remember his arm around my shoulder when I am eight at the Guinness Hall of World Records and we pose for a photograph in front of a statue of the world's tallest man. The guy I see in the coffin has the same soft round face, the same brown dad mustache, and it surprises me that he looks so much like himself, the way I will be surprised years later when I study my own face in the mirror and find it belonging to the face of a forty-year-old husband and father—older than my dad will ever be. Sometimes I see his face in my own, and my own in

my kids'. And sometimes I am overwhelmed with the strange-
ness and suddenness of time, how a lifetime can collapse into
a moment.

The funeral service is quick. I sit in the front row with
Beth and Eric. Susan is not with us because she will not understand. Afterward, people approach to shake our hands and
tell us they are sorry for our loss.

The language of death is curiously proscribed. It is the
one occasion when the spoken word actually resembles the
language of greeting cards. "I'm sorry for your loss." Maybe
it's better to have this script than to allow people to say whatever pops into their heads: "Great funeral. Where're the sand-
wiches?"

When the service is over we get into a limousine for the
long drive to the cemetery. It is the first limousine I have
ever been in, and I have to pretend not to care, but I do care
because it's exciting to drive in a car this big. There are real
glasses lined up along the side, beer and soft drinks on ice.
Beth says we can have a can of Coke if we want. I say no
thanks even though I think it would be pretty cool to sip a
cold Coke from a real glass in a limousine the way I imagine
Billy Joel probably does every day of his life.

Nobody says much as we drive to the cemetery, almost
three hours away near Woodstock. I am bored and watch cars
go by in the other direction. Maybe they are looking at our
small funeral procession and wondering who died. Maybe
they will think it was somebody important.

Somewhere along the New York State Thruway, we pull
over at a rest stop to stretch our legs. There's a small build-

ing with restrooms and vending machines. Eric and I spot a couple of video games shoved in the corner, including a fancy new fighter jet game that costs fifty cents. I notice somebody has already put one quarter in and point out to my brother that if we had another quarter we could play at a significant discount. When Beth comes out of the restroom, Eric tells Beth that I want a quarter to play the video game, and I am filled with shame for thinking about arcade games at a time like this. "Do you want a quarter?" asks Beth.

"No," I say.

"You said you wanted one," says Eric.

"I DID NOT!"

Beth turns and walks back to the car.

"Asshole," I whisper to my brother.

He doesn't respond, but I can tell by his silence that he is pleased with himself for ratting me out, the fucker. He walks to the car behind Beth and I check my pockets one more time to make sure I do not have a quarter.

The cemetery is small and bucolic. It is kind of funny to think of my father, the least cool man on the planet, buried here, so close to Woodstock, the seminal event of coolness for his generation. I doubt he could have named more than one or two popular musicians. The only thing I'd ever heard him listen to on the radio was a show called *What's Your Problem?* hosted by an ancient-sounding guy named Bernard Meltzer, who offered dry legal and financial advice to callers. It is the least entertaining show in the history of radio.

I can't concentrate on the ceremony. Instead I am fascinated by the machine that lowers the coffin into the hole. It's some sort of winch. I've never seen one before and I have an urge to ask how it works, how the cemetery workers retrieve the straps supporting the coffin once it's been fully lowered, if the speed is variable, and whether or not it can also raise coffins. Then it occurs to me that it would be really cool if the winch was powerful enough to not only raise coffins, but fling them.

I spend the rest of the ceremony imagining coffins being flung onto hippies.

Soon the whole thing is over. Dad is buried. We drive home. I return to school.

My best friend Bradley, whom I have not seen since Dad died, strides up to me at the bus stop, holding out his hand for me to shake. "I'm sorry for your loss," he says, the way he was undoubtedly instructed to do by his parents.

How odd, this formality. Two twelve-year-old boys shaking hands at the bus stop. I want to laugh as I pump his hand and say, "Pleasure to make your acquaintance" in a bad British accent. But instead I thank him, then we both kick some wood chips and find ourselves, for the first time in our lives, with nothing to say to each other.

When we get to school, nobody calls me "dead dad kid." It's unclear whether they even noticed I was gone. Movie restrictions are put back in place. The cereal in our cupboard is once again the cereal of lesbians and the constipated. A year later, Beth marries a friend of Dad's who is really into doo-wop music, and they move to Georgia.

A malpractice suit lurches through the court system for years.

For the rest of my childhood, the back of my mind holds the tantalizing promise of blood money. I try not to think about it because it feels dirty and wrong, but I can't help it. What if I wake up one day and I'm rich? What will I do? The answer is obvious: I will buy a black Trans Am like Burt Reynolds had in *Smokey and the Bandit.* Or, perhaps by the time the lawsuit gets settled, there will be jet packs. If so, I will buy one and become awesome. I will also buy a pinball machine and a waterbed.

When the case is finally settled years later, I am an adult, and my brother and I agree to put almost all of the money into a trust for Susan. There will be no jet packs. I will not be awesome.

The other night, I told my son, Elijah, that I would be leaving town for work for a few days. I had been gone for several days the week before, and when I tell him I am leaving again, he starts to cry. (Martha thinks he cries too much; I don't. I cried a lot, too, when I was nine.)

"You're gone too much," he says. He's right. I am.

I tell him I hate leaving so often, but I will be home in a few days and when I get back from this trip, I will be home for several weeks in a row.

"Promise?" he asks.

"I promise," I say.

He hugs me around the neck and says through his tears, "You're the best dad a kid could ever ask for."

It is the kind of thing that would make me turn the channel if I saw a kid say that on TV. But this is my kid and my life and it is such an earnest, heartbreaking moment that I almost burst into tears myself. I mean, doesn't he know what an asshole I am?

Doesn't he know how much I resented him when he was a baby, crying in the night? Or, now that he's older, doesn't he notice when I am so immersed on the computer that I don't listen to the stories he tells me about his day? Doesn't he know that I am sometimes glad to be far away from him and his sister and his mother, all by myself, in a hotel room where nobody needs me for anything? I'm not the best dad a kid could ever ask for. I'm not even close.

I stifle my own tears and hug him back, telling him he's the best son a dad could ever ask for. (I am careful to say he is the best "son" a dad could ever ask for, not the best "kid" because that would imply favoritism with his sister, which would be wrong. Because she *is* my favorite. That was a joke. Now I feel awful for making that joke. Not awful enough to remove it, though. See? Proof that I'm an asshole.) Then I kiss him good night and tell him I love him, just as I have told him every day since he was born.

On the way out of Elijah's bedroom, my mind flashes back to that night when I felt the need to flee my dad's car after telling him I loved him. Now that I am older and a father myself, I find my point of view shifting from me, the child, to imagining myself as my father, in the driver's seat, watching a boy not much older than my son is now, running away, embarrassed. Through the windshield I watch him dash up the sidewalk, and the words lodge in my throat—*I love you, too.* I watch as he disappears into the house, the front door closing behind him.

CHAPTER 10

i hate my baby

We are four months into parenthood and I hate my baby. When friends ask how it is going I always answer the same way: "Terrible." They think I am kidding but I'm not. So far, being a dad sucks.

The main problem is the sleep deprivation. Martha and I are always awake. Every day, all day. I feel as though I have been awake for eight months out of the last four. I have grown to know the wee hours of the night in an intimate and hostile way, the way I might get to know a prison cellmate.

I cannot think. I cannot function. I am suffering. Martha is suffering, too, but I do not care. Right now, I am immune to anybody's suffering but my own. Of course, I knew sleep deprivation would be a problem heading into parenthood, but I did not realize that when people said, "You won't get any sleep," what they were *actually* saying was, "You won't get any sleep."

Elijah almost never stops crying. He cries every night from about ten o'clock until four in the morning. He cries at six-thirty in the morning, again at nine, noon, and periodically throughout the day. Obviously, babies are supposed to cry, but not all the time, right? Why does he cry so much? What does he want? Why is my baby such a dick?

When the middle of the night comes, as it must, and his cries come, as they must, we lie in bed arguing over whose turn it is to get up with the baby. It is always the other person's turn.

"Your turn," we say to each other while he wails.

"Your turn."

"Your turn."

"I got up last time."

"I got up two times in a row before that."

"I'm not getting him."

"I'm not getting him, either."

Ten or twenty minutes might go by like this, neither of us willing to move, the tension growing between us with each wailing exhalation. They say if you just let babies cry, they will eventually cry themselves out. This is not true. Not only will babies not cry themselves out, but the act of crying actually slows down time itself—the more you let them cry, the slower time goes. That's why it took eight months to get through four.

Finally, one of us surrenders, throwing off the warm blankets so as to let as much cold air into the bed as possible. "I hate you," she will say to me or I will say to her, and it won't be said in a whimsical, "aren't we cute," *Ally McBeal* sort of way. The hatred we have for each during those cold hours when somebody must tend to the hellion she created is a visceral, concentrated hate. It is to normal hate what a diamond is to a lump of coal. The only thing preventing us from strangling each other in moments like these is the knowledge that doing so would mean even more time alone with the baby for whichever one of us is left.

"Your turn," says Martha. It is always my turn. GOD DAMN IT! I get up to comfort my stupid baby.

I find him on his back in his crib with his little feet kicking against the air, arms punching, his face splotchy and red like a bruised tomato. I pick him up and feel his lumpy body strain and heave and complain at the injustice of it all. *I know, buddy, I know.*

Each night, I pace the hallway with my son leaning against my shoulder and jiggle him as we walk. "Shh, shh, shh," I whisper in time with my jiggles. "Shh, shh, shh." Sometimes I do it to the tune of "Twinkle, Twinkle, Little Star" or "Mary Had a Little Lamb" or "Mr. Brownstone" by Guns N' Roses—anything to distract myself from the mindless, somnambulistic task at hand.

Constant movement helps. Constant movement and Martha's boobs, which are sore from overuse, her nipples tender and stretched out. They're starting to look like cocktail wieners.

Maybe he's hungry. He can't be hungry. He just fed an hour ago. Maybe he's wet. He's not but I change his diaper anyway. Does he need to burp? Pat, pat, pat, pat, pat. No burp. Burp, damn it! PAT, PAT, PAT! Burp. More crying.

We pace. Pace, pace, pace.

We jiggle. Jiggle, jiggle, jiggle.

I go downstairs and turn on the TV. Every channel is an infomercial. Infomercials for exercise machines and Proactiv acne medication and no-money-down real estate seminars. I used to think that the reason companies showed infomercials in the middle of the night was that that was the only time the companies could afford to buy airtime. Now I know the reason they show them at that hour is because everything looks desirable when you are delirious from fatigue, and the act of picking up a telephone and ordering the Amazing Thigh and Ab Rocker (two easy payments of $19.99) is the closest you will come to human contact. At this hour, the Amazing Thigh and Ab Rocker actually starts to seem like a pretty good solution to most of my problems.

I keep the sound on the television low and jiggle my son. I do loops from kitchen to dining room to living room to kitchen. I cannot look outside because it is like the North Pole in December out there. It is beyond night out there. It is the night of night. It is the kind of postapocalyptic darkness that tells you people are about to start eating other people. Better to close the blinds, stay inside, and spend some quality time with my new friend Body by Jake.

I try my hardest to stay down there, in the radiated darkness, so that Martha can sleep. Eventually, though, his crying drives me back to bed. He wants the boob.

Martha can barely rouse herself to consciousness to give it to him. She turns to her side and lets him suck until he falls, mercifully, to sleep, his little body wedged between us in bed. This presents a new problem; I can never fully fall asleep with him there. I am terrified I will squish him in the middle of the night, flatten him like a cartoon steamroller.

Half an hour later he is up again, crying.

We do our best to cope, but our best is terrible. "You take him!" we shout at each other every twenty minutes when his constant crying has made putty of our brains and we either have to keep passing him back and forth or else throw him out the window.

When I am dragging my feet through our impossibly creaky house I am reminded of something we were taught in the Lamaze class we took. Our instructor, a cheerful and chubby woman named Patti, told us never to shake our baby. This was emphasized several times. "Never shake the baby," she said over and over again.

We even had to watch a video about it. The video showed us what happens when a full-grown adult shakes a newborn. The baby's brain rattles inside its little head like a lump of Silly Putty in its plastic egg. All kinds of terrible things happen as a result. The video shows paralyzed babies and babies with brain injuries and developmental problems and shows us the weeping mother of a baby who died, the result of a boyfriend's bad temper. They have a name for all of this abuse: Shaken Baby Syndrome. It is a curious name to me because the name makes it sound like something that just kind of happens, like a tropical storm.

"Never shake the baby," Patti says again.

God, I want to shake that baby. When he is crying at 3:47 a.m. and he will not shut up, shaking him not only seems like the logical thing to do, it almost feels like the *moral* thing to do. Just a few quick shakes to startle him into silence. How good it would feel to hold him by his little shoulders and rattle him around until he pipes the fuck down.

But I don't do it.

Because I am a saint.

Occasionally, I see an article in the newspaper about parents who abuse their children. Before I had a child, I used to think, *How could this happen?* Now, I find myself wondering why it doesn't happen more often. Why aren't parents throwing their kids into Dumpsters every day? And why, God, why do people have more than one? Because after you've done this once, there can be no possible excuse for doing it again. The thought occurs to me that if parenthood is this hard for everybody, infanticide would be as common as public urination. The human species would have died out long ago. Therefore, our experience cannot be common. Clearly there is either something wrong with us or there is something wrong with him. Maybe our kid is a lemon.

We've been to the doctor several times since his birth for regular checkups. Each time he is pronounced normal. Each time we ask about the crying.

"Colic," says our pediatrician, a round, bearded guy who wears cheery ties featuring paintings of teddy bears. Colic, he explains, is a catch-all term used to describe intestinal distress or abdominal distress or gastric distress. In other words, distress.

"What causes colic?" we ask.

"Nobody knows for sure," he says.

"What can we do?"

"Not much," he says with a chuckle, like we are all in on some big, private joke. There is nothing funny here. I want to strangle him with his stupid teddy bear tie.

He presses his stethoscope against Elijah's chest, pushes into his stomach with a hairy-knuckled finger, and rotates his legs. In this position Elijah looks like a Cornish game hen. The doctor checks his eyes and ears. Of course, now that he is being manhandled by a stranger and has a legitimate excuse to cry, Elijah is calm. He's like a car that only acts up when the mechanic is not around. It's embarrassing. God, I hate my baby.

Dr. Teddy Bear finishes his exam and once again pronounces my son normal. Colicky, but normal.

I suppose most parents would be thrilled with this diagnosis. Not me. I'm pissed off. He can't be normal. He is obviously abnormal. Because we cannot handle this kind of normalcy. There has to be something wrong with him. Nothing too serious. Certainly nothing a series of painful shots won't cure. Maybe rickets. Do babies get rickets?

"What are rickets?" I ask the doctor.

"When will this end?" Martha wants to know.

"Hopefully, soon," he says. He tells us colic almost always resolves itself and we just have to ride it out. Easy for him to say, the quack. He wishes us good luck and leaves the room for his next appointment. As soon as he is out the door, Elijah begins to cry.

We seek advice from every available resource. It turns out there is a whole "Difficult Baby" cottage industry. Hucksters are making millions off desperate people, like ourselves, who will pay any amount for a single moment's rest. Why do none of these people have infomercials on at four o'clock in the morning when they would be most useful?

We buy difficult-baby nutrients. We buy difficult-baby books. We watch difficult-baby videos. We swaddle. We unswaddle. We let him cry. We don't let him cry. We try everything, but nothing helps except jiggling and the boob.

The only other thing he likes is to get out. Away from home, he drinks in the world, watchful and silent. So we take him out as often as we can. To the supermarket, to Starbucks, and for rides in the car where the rhythm and noise conk him out. Often when we are pushing his stroller through another interminable lap around the mall, people stop to tell us what a beautiful and easy baby we have. "Fuck you," I say. (I don't really say, "Fuck you" to these people, but I want to.)

It would help if we had grandparents nearby, somebody to help us shoulder the burden. But my mom is in Florida, and Martha's parents are in Minnesota. There are only the two of us versus this tiny, irascible thing. Two against one. We outweigh him by over two hundred pounds. We are taller and fitter and smarter. And we are losing.

The only respite I get is my job. I am acting part-time on a TV show. Sometimes my days run long, twelve or fourteen hours. Often when I return from work, Martha has not even gotten dressed. Her hair is greasy and tangled and dark winter shadows have settled under her eyes.

"Here," she says, holding the baby out to me like a bag of overripe trash. I take him. She marches upstairs. I hear the bathroom door slam behind her, the sound of shower water running through the pipes.

"Hi, baby," I say, bringing him close. He cries.

All my fears about not measuring up as a father are coming

true. Elijah seems to instinctively know I am not to be trusted. He senses that I am somehow going to screw up his entire childhood, the way an animal can detect an earthquake before it arrives.

The rational part of my brain understands that of course Elijah prefers his mother. After all, until recently she was the only home he ever knew. Plus, she supplies most of his food and smells good (at least when she showers, which isn't that often these days). Babies *should* gravitate toward their mothers; this seems natural and right.

But the emotional part of my brain feels betrayed. Doesn't he know how amusing I am? How good I am at Scrabble? I want to tell him that if he will just give me a chance I will do right by him. I will push him in his baby swing and give him the last piece of pizza and help him with his homework and talk to him about girls (or boys, if it comes to that), that I will spring for guitar lessons and teach him how to skateboard. I want to tell him that I will always buy him the correct baseball mitt.

Instead, I say the only thing I can think of to say in this moment: "Please, please, please shut up."

Is he occasionally cute? Sure. Like all parents, we marvel at him when he does his amazing baby tricks. He wriggles and coos and does all the de rigueur baby things. He breaks into wide gummy smiles when I splutter kisses against his tummy. He likes bouncing in the filthy plastic saucer we stole from the town dump.

We tell ourselves his crying jags probably indicate unusual intelligence. "Of course he's crying," we say to each other. "He's smart. He needs constant stimulation." When I research this topic online, I do not find a correlation between colic and genius, although I do discover a study from the University of Iowa that shows a relationship between "early fussiness" and "later psychiatric problems."

There is nothing to do except tell ourselves we will get through this. It is the only lie we have left.

One night, we put him into his crib around ten and race each other into bed because we know he will be up soon. I fall asleep and awaken, as always, to his cries.

"Your turn," Martha says.

I open my eyes. Something is wrong, although I cannot immediately place the problem. Then I realize: it's the sun. I can see sunlight. I look at my bedside clock: 5:24 a.m. My God, it's morning. He slept through the night. Seven and a half hours of uninterrupted sleep. Oh my God, I just got a full night's sleep.

Scooping him from his crib, I rush downstairs, swirl together a bottle for him, and plant him in his grubby play saucer. I make eggs. I do jumping jacks. I punch the air in celebration. A car drives by. Other people are awake! My kid slept through the night. He is the best baby in the world. I love my baby.

The next night, he wakes up fifteen times.

Even so, it feels like a fever has broken in our home. If he can sleep through the night once, he can do it again. Over time, he does. A night here, a night there. After about eight months, he is doing it on a more or less regular basis. 5:24 a.m. is still a barbaric time of day, but compared to 3:47 a.m., it actually looks pretty good.

Several years later, the Abu Ghraib torture scandal explodes. Reading the accounts of the abuse toward prisoners, it strikes me how much the experiences of the Iraqi prisoners mirrored my own in those days. Consider what the prisoners were made to endure:

- Sleep deprivation
- Stress positions
- Unceasing, annoying sounds
- Intimidation by dogs (Our hyperactive puppy, Lily, a yellow Labrador retriever, is a constant drain on whatever stores of energy the kid has not already sapped from us. I hate my puppy.)
- Humiliating photographic evidence of abuse

There is a picture Martha took of me during this time in our lives. I am in our backyard raking leaves. Elijah is strapped to me in a BabyBjörn, his fat little body dangling from my sternum. My hair has the rangy texture of a feral cat. My complexion is sallow, jaundiced. I hold a rake in my hand, surrounded by leaves. Leaves everywhere; I look as if I have been photographed at the beginning of an impossible task. Elijah and I stare at the camera, the same blank, expressionless look on our faces. His face looks like that because he is a baby. Mine does because I am dead.

I look just like those guys in Abu Ghraib. Am I honestly comparing being the parent of a newborn to being a tortured prisoner of war? Obviously not. Being the parent of a colicky newborn, I am convinced, is worse. I am never, ever doing this again.

CHAPTER 11

baby jail

We're having another baby.

This was not the plan. I mean, yes, it was the plan in the sense that we were trying to make another baby, but it was *not* the plan in the sense that I did not expect us to succeed so soon. The first time, it took six months of sustained effort to impregnate Martha with Elijah, back when we were childless and had nothing to do all day but engage in clinical, unappealing lovemaking.

Now we have an eighteen-month-old child who demands every second of our attention. There is never a moment in the day when we are not tending to him in some capacity. Elijah is up on his feet, stumbling through each day on chubby legs, endlessly seeking ways to cause his own destruction. It seems like a mistake of nature that children learn to walk before they learn to speak. The words "Don't put the electrical cord in your mouth" mean nothing to him. We are in a perpetual state of high alert, always on the balls of our feet, arms forever outstretched in his direction, attempting to anticipate his next suicidal impulse.

By the time we get him into his crib each night we are both wiped out. Less so now that he sleeps through the night, but enough so that the last thing either of us wants to do in our free time is to expend more energy on something as frivolous as creating a new life. But we need to try now because we want our children to be close enough in age so that they can be playmates. This will be fun for them, but more important, it will be fun for us, since it will hopefully mean we have to play with them less.

Playing with kids, even your own, is a bore. Children are terrible playmates. The games they play are no fun and neither are the rules they invent. If at any time things are not going their way, they change the no-fun rules into even-less-fun rules that favor them. It's tedious. I only enjoy playing with my own kid for five minutes at a time. I defy any adult of normal intelligence to play peek-a-boo for longer than that without experiencing irrepressible fury.

I am no more ready to make Baby #2 than I was with Baby #1. I console myself with the belief that I've got a good six months or more ahead of me before pregnancy becomes a reality. It took that long the first time around, and now that we have less time and energy to do the deed, it will almost certainly take even longer.

During our first month trying to conceive, we only manage to have sex a single time. Having sex once a month is bad even if a couple is *not* trying to make a baby. For a couple attempting to transform egg to embryo, it's terrible. Maybe subconsciously we are trying to minimize the chance that Martha will actually get pregnant. Or maybe we are just not attracted to each other right now. Whatever the reason, if we're going to have any hope of getting this thing done before Elijah graduates from high school, we're going to have to get our numbers up.

A couple of weeks later Martha walks into my office, where I am working at my new desk, and says, "I'm pregnant."

"No way."

She holds up a pee stick. Two lines. She's pregnant.

"I'm so happy," I say. I am not happy.

Shit! I thought we were just having warm-up sex! The first month is batting practice. That's when we're supposed to get out on the field and take a few practice swings. That's it! I didn't even think it was possible to make a baby the first time up at bat. Obviously, yes, I know that health teachers everywhere warn teenagers that they can become pregnant their very first time having sex, but I always figured those were just scare tactics.

What happened to my lazy, unmotivated, good-for-nothing, shiftless sperm with unimpressive motility? Now, suddenly, my sperm are up-and-at-'em? C'mon guys, let's try to all get on the same page here!

Her pregnancy is worse the second time around. She is nauseous all the time, except that now she cannot just go lie down when she feels bad, because we have a toddler who demands her full-time attention and he does not give a shit about Mommy's "throw-up time." He wants his Cheerios and his ba-ba (bottle) and his Thomas the Fucking Tank Engine and he wants it all tout de suite.

Martha shows earlier this time. Her tummy pops out and she makes me touch her stomach every time the baby does anything. There is something unnerving to me about touching a creature living within my wife. I didn't like it with Elijah and I don't like it with this new thing.

"That's a foot," she says, as a little lump percolates up from her torso.

"Okay, I get it," I say.

Like with Elijah, we decide to wait to find out the baby's gender. I don't know why, but it feels more organic or something. When people ask me what I'm hoping for, I have a standard joke: "I don't care what sex it is," I say, "as long as it's gorgeous."

Nobody ever finds this joke as funny as I do.

Although my attitude is better this time around, the further into the pregnancy we get, the more scared I become. Last time I was scared because I did not know what I was getting into. This time I'm scared because I know *exactly* what I'm getting into. What if we have a second colicky baby? How could we possibly survive that?

Everybody tells us that won't happen. "There's no way," they say.

We tell each other the same thing. It seems so statistically improbable as to be meaningless. Having another baby as difficult as Elijah would be like being in two plane crashes. Granted, a much higher percentage of babies develop colic than airplanes develop catastrophic engine failure, but still, we're not *that* unlucky. "There's no way," we tell each other.

You're probably thinking, *I bet their second baby was just as bad as the first.* But you would be wrong to make that assumption. Our second baby is not as bad as Elijah.

She is worse.

Ruth Maxine Black is born in May of the following year after a comparatively easy delivery. A little IV, a little epidural, some Pitocin, and bang! Baby. Martha is so relaxed, she actually asked for a mirror to be held up between her legs so she could watch the delivery. We watch her head emerge, her shoulders and back, and finally her fat marshmallow butt before she wriggles free. "It's a girl," says the doctor.

"Are you sure?" asks Martha, which strikes me as kind of funny because it seems that one of the first things they would teach students at medical school is how to tell boys from girls. If he isn't sure at this point, he should probably consider another profession.

We're thrilled to have a little girl. When she comes home, she sleeps a lot, just as babies are supposed to do. We congratulate ourselves for having such an easy baby this time around. We have made two perfect children, one of each sex. We are amazing parents.

Two weeks later the colic bomb goes off. It's the same deal as with Elijah, only worse because now we have this shitty stupid two-year-old who doesn't understand what the hell just happened to his life. Why is there a baby in his house? Why isn't Mama giving him as much attention? He pouts through his days, sullen and prone to tears.

I feel terrible for my son and try to give him comfort. We go out together to do guy stuff. Guy stuff means going to the local Barnes & Noble where they've got a Thomas the

Tank Engine train table set up. I sit there for hours as he runs Thomas, Edward, Percy, and Henry across the Isle of Sodor. If that sounds boring, let me assure you that it is.

One upshot of this go-round is that I am regularly getting a full night's sleep because we agreed that I would sleep in the guest room for the first couple of months. Martha takes Ruthie during the night. At dawn, I take her and Elijah together so that Martha can grab a few hours of uninterrupted sleep before starting her day. The system is working out better for both of us, but a better version of terrible is still terrible.

The fatigue reawakens all the scary fantasies I used to have of harming my child. One morning, I am so frustrated and angry when Ruthie refuses to take her bottle that I whip it across the room as hard as I can, splattering formula everywhere and creating a satisfying divot in the drywall. Scarier still is the fact that I don't love this new baby. Not even a little bit. Not now, not when she is a lumpy and hateful annoyance who won't let me hold her, cries when she sees me, and generally likes me even less than Elijah did when he was born. Some people would probably make the argument that love is a two-way street, and that the reason Ruthie doesn't react better to me is that she can sense my resentment and antipathy toward her. To those people I would say this: Shut up.

My early emotional indifference, I think, must be common among new parents, although nobody wants to talk about it. There is an assumption that all parents fall head over heels in love with their kids as soon as they emerge from the womb. Not me. I didn't with Elijah and I don't with this new one.

Maybe mothers are more likely to bond with their kids right away; actually growing a kid inside their bodies and carrying it around for months must create an emotional bond to accompany the physical one. I understand; whenever we plant carrots during the summer, I feel far more affection for the carrots we grow than the ones we buy. Same thing with kids.

Ruthie will not stop screaming. Any good feelings I had about this child right after her birth, the lovely scene where I was in the delivery room with my wife, tears trickling down my cheeks, aflush with all that miracle-of-life hooey, all those feelings are gone. Now I am up at dawn with a crying newborn and a restless, mopey toddler. That awful feeling of sleep deprivation has returned and settled deep into my limbs, making them heavy and unresponsive. I feel like I am living in a big pot of cauliflower-and-dick soup.

My only consolation, if there is one, is that I have already experienced this once with Elijah, so I know, somewhere in the back of the reptilian part of my brain that I depend on for survival, that this too shall pass. Ruth will eventually sleep through the night. She will eventually stop crying *all the time*. She will. Right? I have to cling to this hope because hope is the only thing sustaining me right now.

Martha and I are also in survival mode as a couple, sailors on a capsizing ship. The only way for us to stay afloat is to focus on simple daily tasks. Laundry, changing the Diaper Genie, grocery shopping, burping the baby, cleaning the house, bathing the children and ourselves, feeding the children and ourselves, and always, rocking the baby, rocking the baby, rocking the baby. We are in baby jail.

It takes four months for Ruthie to sleep through the night, just as it did with Elijah, and another eight for the colic to fully disappear. What finally emerges is a lovely little girl who enjoys painting and princesses and farts. Over time, as the kids get more independent, the stress of parenting eases up a bit. We are still in baby jail, but we have been moved to a better cell block. Over time, our jailers give us more and more freedom. Now that the kids are older, I would say we are in a minimum-security facility; we are even allowed the occasional conjugal visit. From time to time, Martha and I talk about having a third kid, the way old prisoners talk about taking down one last score. But we're all talk. Our marriage wouldn't survive another baby. Having barely survived two colicky babies, Martha and I are scared straight.

CHAPTER 12

a little hard work

During my parents' breakup, I remember both of them emphasizing several times that their divorce was not my fault. It was a funny thing to hear because until they started reassuring me that it wasn't my fault, it had never occurred to me that it was. Their assurances had the opposite effect than what they intended. I mean, if you tell somebody enough times that something isn't their fault, eventually that person will start to think, *Maybe this is all my fault.*

But, of course, my parents' divorce had nothing to do with me. It was my brother's fault. (That's a joke.) No, the blame lay entirely with them, two people who never should have married in the first place. Mom and Dad met as students at Indiana University. Even though both were city kids—Mom from Chicago, Dad from Brooklyn—they had each led sheltered lives to that point. Both were quiet, studious Jewish kids—"goody-goodies," as my mother says. Neither had much experience dating, and I suspect they convinced themselves they were in love because it seemed like the logical progression of their relationship. I imagine their early love to be sweet and trusting and naïve, the kind of love that sees possibilities beyond what a clear-headed assessment of their compatibility would merit—such as the facts that my father was a borderline Asperger's case, and my mother a closeted lesbian.

They married in a windowless Chicago hotel ballroom in 1968. In the few photos I have from the wedding, the women wear beehive hairdos and cat-eye glasses. The men are doughy, and each one looks as if he is one helping of beef stroganoff away from a massive coronary. The entire affair seems as much like a bowling league awards night as a wedding. It is a smoky world of clumpy dresses and trousers cinched too tight.

I wish I could say Mom and Dad look happy in those photos, but to my eye they do not. They look young and nervous. Yes, they are smiling as they cut the cake, smiling as they pose with their families, my mother smiles as she walks down the aisle in her slim white wedding dress. But their smiles have a starchy determination, something stuck in place, like hair spray. Every caption of their wedding photos could read, "What the hell are we doing?"

I understand the feeling.

After a lot of yelling and trial separations, they broke up for good eight years and three kids later. It was an acidic, drawn-out divorce followed by years of bitterness that still hadn't healed by the time my dad died. After it was finalized, I never heard my mom say anything nice about my father, and I never heard him speak of her at all.

Nearly everybody I knew came from a divorced household. Among my friends, having divorced parents was as common as having an Atari 2600. Those parents who remained married didn't seem particularly happy. The one exception I can remember is my friend Kip, whose folks appeared to still be in love after three kids and fifteen years together. But Kip's parents were stoners who ran a homemade chocolate business out of their kitchen. Also, I think they might have been swingers.

Even though I didn't have a lot of firsthand evidence around me to suggest that marriage was worthwhile, in my heart of hearts I am a traditional man. I like traditional things: domesticity, a wood-burning fireplace, good old-fashioned masturbation. Marriage fits right onto that list. The idea of marriage is so appealing. You pick somebody out, say your "I do's," build a family, then sit on the couch and wait for each other to die. Perfect.

Back when we all died young and beautiful (or at least young), marriage was easier to sustain. By the time you'd grown tired of each other, one of you probably had tuberculosis anyway. Now that we're all living so long, the idea of looking at the same person every day for fifty or sixty years might be more than our species is equipped to handle.

"You again?"

"Yes, me. Me for the rest of your medically extended life."

The other night after the kids went to bed, Martha and I are watching TV in the living room when she turns to me and says, "I'm not sure I believe people should stay married forever. I think maybe twelve or fifteen years is enough. You should get married for a little while, then at a certain point, move on."

We have been married thirteen years, exactly within the time frame Martha has just defined as the point when people should split up.

"Are you saying you want to get divorced?" I ask her.

"Not right now," she says, turning back to the TV.

This is not our first conversation about divorce. We talk about it all the time. Martha and I discuss divorce the way other couples discuss vacation plans: *I hear divorce is beautiful this time of year.* In our case, divorce isn't imminent. It's just one of those things we daydream about. One of the unexpected joys of being married is the hours of fantasizing it allows me to do about how much better my life would be if I got divorced.

Bachelorhood would be an endless Frank Sinatra song. Booze and dames, dames and booze (or, if not booze, then at least well-carbonated soft drinks). I'd spend my nights hitting on stewardesses at swanky nightspots like Applebee's. It would be grand.

"Buy you a drink?" I'd say to whichever foxy lady caught my eye. Before she could respond, I'd call to the bartender: "Al! A martini for the lady. And another Diet Pepsi for me."

Al would bring the cocktails. There'd be a little flirty contretemps.

"I ought to throw this in your face," she might say.

"Good. I could use a little cooling off."

We'd toss back our cocktails. We'd rumba. Then we'd have sex. My divorce fantasies always end with me banging a stewardess. Or a nurse. Or anybody with a vagina.

The frequency and intensity of these fantasies waxes and

wanes along with my marriage's peculiar biorhythms. Contentedness, remorse. Contentedness, remorse. We go through these cycles over and over again, sometimes within the same day. Sometimes within the same hour.

During the bad periods, we fight about everything: housework, child care, my work, my lack of appreciation for her, her lack of appreciation for me, my irresponsibility, her anxiety, her opinion that I'm not home enough and when I'm home I'm not doing enough, my opinion that she doesn't understand that when I leave it's because I have to make money for us and it's not fair that she should get mad at me for going to my "job," which I put in quotes because *she* puts the word in quotes with her tone, as if the fact that I enjoy what I do for a living disqualifies it from being actual work because she is not experiencing boundless joy in her current position of "wife and mother."

Sometimes weeks drizzle by like this, weeks where a persistent, dissolute pitter-patter beats down on our heads, each moment another drop in the Chinese water torture that is our marriage. These are weeks when we barely speak and do not touch and any attempt at reconciliation ends up causing more fights. It is during these periods when those distant nights at Applebee's loom just a little closer. It's not even that we're mad at each other exactly. It's that we just have to see each other's fucking faces every fucking day.

If we ever do split up, the end of our marriage will most likely be less about each other and more about the simple fact that marriage sometimes sucks. Nobody told me this before I got married. People hinted at it, but the closest anybody got to actually spelling out how difficult marriage can be were the ones who euphemistically warned me that "marriage is a lot of hard work."

That's okay, I thought to myself, *I'm not afraid of a little hard work.* At the time, my job was writing sketches for a TV show, so I did not have the broadest perspective on what constituted "hard work." For me, a bad day on the job was when a joke didn't get a laugh. As far as bad days on the job go, that doesn't really rate. For some people, a bad day at work is when an oil rig explodes.

A bad day in marriage is when, after a furious argument with your wife over your lack of attention to detail when cleaning the mashed potatoes out of a pot, you attempt to pull the stainless-steel rack of kitchen utensils out of the wall for the purpose of throwing it across the room, but cannot do so because you lack the upper body strength to dislodge the goddamned thing from the drywall screws holding it in place, so instead you pull at it and pull at it without result until you are so embarrassed at your lack of manliness that you scream something unintelligible before storming out of the house and driving your car around in circles for five hours because you feel too angry and ashamed to go home and face the woman to whom you have, bewilderingly, committed your life.

(In the above example, you = me.)

Somebody really should warn potential spouses that marriage is more taxing than the normal definition of "hard work." Vows about "honoring" and "cherishing" are great, but I would suggest that after all the flowery stuff and the "love is patient and kind" biblical verses, officiants should end wedding ceremonies with the words, "And you know marriage sucks, right?"

"I do."

That way, at least it's on record. If wedding vows were phrased that way, maybe fewer people would sign up. It cannot be a coincidence that the word we most often use to describe marriage, *institution,* is also the word we use for the place we put crazy people.

I'm not saying marriage sucks *all* the time, not even *most* of the time. But it sucks enough of the time that people should enter into it with the expectation that there is going to be a fair amount of suckiness involved. The suckiness usually isn't even anybody's fault. Both bride and groom enter marriage wishing for happiness and success. Both generally do their best. So why do marriages fail half the time? My theory is that the problem is not with the people, but with the concept itself. Consider the difference between the following two sentences:

"Hey, you wanna hang out?"

"Hey, you wanna hang out *forever?*"

Martha and I recently had a massive, blowout fight about her insistence on keeping the bedroom clock radio set ten minutes fast.

Her: "Setting the clock like this helps me stay on time!"

Me: "But if you know it's ten minutes fast, you're just telling yourself a lie that you already know is a lie! You're not fooling yourself."

Her: "It helps me!"

Me: "But when the clock is fast I get confused!"

(I would like to emphasize that one of my arguments to her is "I get confused.")

Yes, during that fight she told me she hated me. The phrase, "You have lost the right to speak to me for the rest of the weekend" was uttered by one of us. (Her.)

Yes, I responded in the infuriating way I do, with big silent eyes that are meant to say, "You are a crazy person," the result of which is only to make her crazier.

Yes, our daughter screamed to us in tears from her bedroom, "Stop fighting! Stop fighting!" over and over again.

Yes, we ignored her and continued fighting about the clock radio for another two hours. Martha played the divorce card, as she always does, within the first five minutes of our fight.

"I don't know why I ever married you!" Martha screamed at me. "We should just get divorced!"

"Call a lawyer!" I screamed back.

No, we did not subsequently laugh about the whole silly fight and then make love.

When we have arguments like that we are so focused on proving our own rightness that neither of us can see any humor in the situation. We do this all the time, this endless cycle of accusation and counteraccusation. Over the years we have piled so many grievances upon each other that sometimes I feel like we are turning into those hoarders on TV who cannot step in any part of their home without fear that their mountainous heaps of junk will collapse upon them.

Some examples of the wrongs over the last decade or so that we have compiled: The time I did not prepare well enough for camping. The time she read my journal without my permission. The time I said I would fertilize the lawn in the fall but waited too long and crabgrass grew in the patchy areas the following spring. The time she could not figure out how to load her CDs onto iTunes and still could not figure it out even after I showed her fifty times, which resulted in a fight about how she never listens and I have no patience. The time she got mad at me for pouting after she asked me to move the outdoor furniture indoors for the winter when I was *very* busy playing *Rock Band 2* on the Wii. All the times I did not see the dog hair on the floor: "How can you not *see* that?"

"I didn't see it."

"You didn't *want* to see it," she says, condemning both my character and my eyesight.

There are only a few options to free ourselves from these self-destructive cycles. The first is that, eventually, one of us will just surrender to the other one. The result would be a lifeless marriage in which one of us just acquiesces to the other one in all matters, a "yes dear" marriage. I couldn't live with myself if I ever did that, although it would be great if she did.

The second solution, sometimes glittering in its attractiveness, is divorce. But even though I occasionally (often) have lengthy fantasies about life as a single man, I do not want to get divorced. Because I love my wife, yes. But also because I have survived the shrapnel from a divorce and know the pain it causes. The act of blowing up marriages has become so routine in our culture that we don't even really think about the effects, but I do not want to ever inflict that kind of damage on the kids, Martha, or myself.

Also, divorce is expensive and I value money more than

I value happiness. I love money. Which is a terrible thing for a Jew to admit since it just reinforces all the stereotypes. But I can't help it. Because just as sometimes Russian female basketball teams really are drunks, sometimes Jews love money.

The final option is to enter therapy. She is the one who first suggests it after another one of our more colorful discussions. I have always resisted therapy based on the theory that people should be able to solve their own damn problems. And also on the theory that I don't want to pay a therapist. But after too many years of bickering with Martha, too many years of being unable to figure out how to quit sequencing through the noisy octaves of our relationship, I come to realize that some problems are beyond my fixing. Even so, I am reluctant to get help.

Because how do you solve yourself?

CHAPTER 13

a perfect date

We find our therapist, Suzy, through a friend who was experiencing similar marital problems as ours. The friend credits Suzy with keeping her marriage intact, which is encouraging because our friend's marriage *really* sucks.

This is a few years ago, when the kids are four and two. At the time, Martha and I are suffering through our sentence in baby jail, both exhausted from chasing children, picking up after children, cleaning the perpetually dirty butts of children. Our marriage has become an interminable to-do list of chores. Parenting feels like a job sorting endless amounts of mail at the post office. The only difference is that, when you work at the post office, you go home at the end of the day. Right now, it feels like when I am done with my job at the post office I go to another post office.

I am reluctant to go when she first suggests couples counseling, but after some hemming and hawing I agree to give it a try since we are both suffering so much that I will do anything to alleviate the pain, even if it means talking to my wife.

The other reason I agree to try therapy is that, in my heart, I feel that after listening to the nature of our disagreements, any qualified therapist will come to the conclusion that I am right about pretty much everything. When I lay out my grievances, I am positive any therapist worth her salt will say, "I agree with Michael."

"But . . . but . . . ," Martha will splutter.

"I'm sorry, Martha. But Michael is right. As far as I can tell, he's always right."

Our first appointment with Suzy is on a drizzly spring day. We drive the fifteen minutes to her office in silence, watching the rain, keeping time to the windshield wipers. Suzy lives on a wooded property and works out of an old yellow barn beside her house. In addition to serving as her office, the barn is also used as a rehearsal space for local dancers. I worry it will smell like incense and/or feet. There is no waiting room, so we wait in tense silence for her to fetch us from the car.

I play with the radio. Martha asks me to stop playing with the radio. I do not stop. She asks me again to stop playing with the radio. I do not stop. Why does she get to control the radio? We're both in the car. Why does her right to silence trump my right to listen to music? Hell no, I'm not turning off the radio. And this is why we are going to get divorced.

Suzy emerges from the barn with another client, a woman a little older than us who looks like she's been crying. Why is she crying? Is she getting divorced? Is this what divorce looks like? I feel compelled to make eye contact with this woman. I'm not sure why. The generous explanation is I want to give her a reassuring smile, a small gift from a stranger. The less generous explanation is that I want to measure her pain against my own, to project myself into her place to see if I could handle whatever suffering she is enduring. The woman climbs into her SUV and drives away without meeting my eyes. Way to leave me hanging, lady.

Suzy waves us over. She is a small woman, around fifty, in loose cotton clothes and chunky jewelry. She's got frizzy black hair streaked with gray. Her vibe is "cool high school English teacher," the kind you might find yourself smoking a joint with a few years after graduation.

After we introduce ourselves, Suzy leads us into the barn (which, to my relief, smells fine) and asks why we are there. *Because she's a fucking bitch* doesn't seem like the right way to kick things off, so I volunteer that we have been fighting a lot.

Suzy asks for specifics. What are we fighting about?

"Money," says Martha.

True dat. Money is a constant flash point between us since we have very different attitudes about its purpose. Martha is of the opinion that money is to be spent in order to create a better life for herself and her loved ones, whereas I am of the opinion that money is a means of keeping score. The more you have, the more you are winning. Winning what? Just winning. Isn't that enough?

"So you're fighting about money," Suzy asks.

"Yes," replies Martha. "And also everything else."

"Let's start with money," Suzy says.

So that's how we start. Right away I like Suzy's style. Unlike some other therapists I've seen, Suzy is a talker. I've never understood those bobblehead therapists who do nothing but nod. It's really annoying. You talk, they nod. Even if you ask them a direct question, they just turn it around. "So what do you think I should do?"

"What do *you* think you should do?"

"I don't know. That's why I'm here."

"Let's explore that."

"Eat me. Is that something we can explore?"

But Suzy is an active participant in the conversation. Instead of sympathetic nods and platitudes, she gives us practical, useful advice. Which is great because that's what I'm paying for. Yes, we need to work on things ourselves, but if she can fast-track the process by telling us we're idiots in one session instead of waiting for us to figure it out in three, that saves us a lot of money, which, as you know, I love.

One hour with Suzy is obviously not enough to dig very deep, but the simple act of frank conversation leaves Martha and me both feeling better. It is the first good talk we have had in weeks. After our session, we treat ourselves to lunch at a nearby restaurant, where we continue talking. So begins a positive feedback loop: therapy leads to good feelings, which leads to lunch, which leads to more conversation, which leads to more therapy, which leads to more lunch.

The lesson: the more you eat, the better you feel.

We see Suzy every week for the next several months. What began as a conversation about money evolves into long and intimate discussions about our deeper selves, the kinds of talks Martha and I used to have on the phone when we were first sneaking around together. The difference is none of these conversations ends with phone sex.

The main thing I take away from those initial sessions is that I can be a real asshole. I knew that already, but to hear my actions reflected back at me from Martha's point of view opens my eyes a bit wider to my sometimes horrible behavior.

Until then, even though I recognized many of my imperfections, I still considered myself to be the hero of a magnificent, epic story in which I starred, a story in which the hero (me) may do some confounding and upsetting things, but his actions are redeemed in the audience's mind because they understand that he is the most fascinating of archetypes, the charming rogue. You know, like Han Solo.

Apparently, the problem with this sort of thinking is that there is no unseen audience. As my therapist pointed out to me, there is nobody out there cheering me on when I call my wife a cunt. (I have called Martha this on at least a couple of occasions. Not proud of it, but there it is. Once I said she was being "cunty," which felt like less of an insult. She did not think so. It should be pointed out, though, that she *was* acting kind of cunty.)

What I learn, and this is a tough pill to swallow, is that other people have their own stories in which I am *not* the star. From their point of view, whenever I do upsetting things, I am less like Harrison Ford as Han Solo and more like Mel Gibson as Mel Gibson.

In fact, Martha stars in her own story, and in *her* story, when I tell her that no, I am not going to clean the bathroom because *I* think cleaning it once every couple of months is plenty so if she wants the bathroom cleaned she can clean it her damned self, she does not interpret my position as that of the common man taking a heroic stand against tyranny. Martha's audience just thinks Martha married a dickhead.

Which maybe she did.

So I'm sure she feels vindicated when I agree with her that much of my behavior is childish and needs to be addressed. But I bet she was not anticipating the degree to which our sessions would end up focusing on *her*. Until now, so much of what was wrong with us as a couple was laid in my lap: *my* depression, *my* stubbornness, *my* sullen attitude and general lack of cooperation.

Now, though, we find ourselves mapping the vast and uncharted territories of Martha's psyche. After much exploration, here is what we discover: Martha is batshit crazy. Obviously, Suzy doesn't use those words, but I do notice that whenever Martha is talking, she uses her finger to make whirling "koo-koo" motions.

Whole sessions with Suzy go by where we talk only about Martha, entire luxurious hours spent chronicling my wife's need to set the house alarm at night and then recheck the alarm to make sure it's set five minutes later, and five minutes after that, and how her newly diagnosed ADD relates to her childhood. I love it. I just get to sit there and make the same kind of nodding motions I hate so much when directed at me. *Yes,* I nod, as she unburdens herself to Suzy. *Yes, I understand.* I press my lips together in a tight sympathetic smile, nodding my bobblehead up and down. *Yes, yes, yes.* I murmur comforting noises and hold her hand, and think about where we will be going for lunch.

It is a perfect date.

Here's the thing: I *do* understand. I know what it's like to tease out your own ugliness and hold it up to the light for examination like a particularly stringy booger you just pulled from your nose. It's gross, certainly, but that's all it is, just something unpleasant we each have within us. All this pain we hold on to, Martha and me, all these fights, the bickering, all of it, is nothing. It's just us saying the same thing over and over again: "I feel alone." The girl sitting next to me struggling to articulate her pain is the girl I love. I miss the girl who does silly dances when Madonna comes on the radio and I miss the boy who danced along when I was twenty-three and falling in love.

How did I end up shrouding my best self in this marriage? When did our definition of ourselves as a couple become about the things we had to do instead of the people we want to be? When did I become afraid to poke fun at her the way I used to, to speak to waiters in funny accents to make her laugh, to buy her huge plastic butterfly key chains with her initials engraved in them just because they were ridiculous? When did that stuff stop? And why?

Fear maybe. The fear that the people we wish ourselves to be, the faces we present to the world, aren't who we really are. That our true selves are the monsters who wear our clothes when we are home. Those other people, the charismatic people we show to the world, where do they go? Do we put them away like the good china, only to be brought out on special occasions? Because that seems like a stupid way to run a life.

I know her better than I have ever known anybody, but there are times when I have also never felt more distant from another person. The thing nobody ever tells you about marriage is that sometimes it makes you lonelier than being alone ever could.

So there we are, week after week, sitting in the corner of a big yellow barn telling a stranger all the things we struggle to say to each other. It helps. The girl I love is there, buried under to-do lists and anxiety, but she's in there. The boy she loves is there, too, overwhelmed and not understanding how he will keep this life going for the people he loves, but he is there. Sometimes when we leave the barn, I feel like I have just stepped out of one of those fancy showers that shoots water at you from a thousand different directions. I feel clean and hopeful and a little aroused.

Sometimes our good feelings carry over the entire week. But sometimes we start screaming at each other again as soon as we get home. That's just the way it goes with us. One step forward, ninety-two steps back.

Over time we do get better. The amount of time between fights lengthens. We are more patient with each other, slower to react to provocation. We practice the listening techniques Suzy teaches us, like repeating back to the other person what they are saying so they feel heard.

Martha: "I feel like you're not helping out enough around the house."

Me: "You feel like I'm not helping out enough around the house."

Martha: "Exactly."

This shit is easy!

Sometimes when she asks me to do something, I don't

even bother repeating it back it to her, or tell her to fucking do it herself. I just do what she asks, without complaint. When I do, I hear my imaginary audience applaud. Once in a while I even hear them say saucy things to me like, "You go, girl!"

A few weeks ago was our anniversary. To celebrate we went to our favorite New York restaurant, Gramercy Tavern. (Reservations: 212-477-0777. In exchange for plugging their restaurant, I will be glad to accept a free dinner from them. Thanks in advance, Gramercy Tavern.) We go there almost every year. When the waiter came to our table, he said, "I think I waited on you guys last year at this same table. Happy anniversary."

I said, "Oh yeah!" like I remembered him. But I didn't remember because I don't remember things. But I was impressed with his memory. (This did not translate to a larger tip for him, by the way, because 5 percent should be enough for any man.) It was nice to be remembered, nicer still to be remembered as a couple. Over the next several hours, we filled ourselves with meats and fish and bread and stinky cheeses. We talked in the easy way we do when we are getting along. We toasted each other with champagne. We laughed. It felt familiar and good, this annual ritual with my wife. Better even than picking up a stewardess at Applebee's.

After dinner we go to a hotel room I've reserved. The kids are home with a babysitter. We have the whole night to ourselves in New York, a rare treat. We undress and contemplate making love, even though we are both so full we feel like pumpkins stuffed with turduckens. Ultimately, we decide against it because one or both of us might barf. Instead, we just lie down beside each other on the bed and kiss. I tell her I love her. I wait for her to tell me she loves me too.

I see her eyes drift to the window.

"What's that?" she says, pointing to the drape. I hear the familiar anxiety in her voice and I tense. Why does she always think something is wrong when nothing is wrong? Why does she worry so much when there is nothing to worry about? She gets up from the bed and walks over to the window. "Oh no."

I sigh and follow her, preparing to tell her that whatever she imagined she saw is nothing, to come back to bed, to kiss me again and tell me she loves me. And, failing that, to tell her she is crazy and needs serious psychiatric help, which probably goes against what Suzy would advise. But when I look at where she's pointing, I realize I cannot tell her these things because crawling across the drapery is a bright red insect the size of a poodle.

"Is that a bedbug?" Martha asks.

"I'm sure it's not," I say.

But my assurances mean nothing to her. New York is currently experiencing an infestation of the little fuckers. We Google "bedbugs" and compare the images we find to the thing in front of us. It's a bedbug.

"We can't stay here," she says.

No, we can stay here! We can just pluck the bedbug from the curtains and flush it down the toilet. We don't even have to sleep in the bed; we can sleep in the bathtub! Don't let one tiny bedbug ruin our night! Let's just be together tonight, here, alone. C'mon!

But no. She's right. We're not staying in this filthy shithole. We have to get out of here. Now. We pack our things as quickly as we can and hightail it out of the hotel, stopping at the lobby to complain to the blank-faced desk clerk.

"Bedbugs!" I yell.

"Ooooh," he says.

"I'm not paying for the room!"

"Ooooh," he says. I don't think he speaks English.

We pick up the car at the garage for the long, late-night drive back to the wilds of Connecticut. We try to laugh about it, but it doesn't feel that funny when it is two o'clock in the morning and we are still a little drunk and carsick from the windy back roads. Anniversary officially ruined. Mood officially soured. She falls asleep in the car, and when we get back a couple of hours later we send the babysitter home, and wake up with the kids at dawn. We are exhausted and snappish with each other the whole next day. When she asks me to take out the garbage I tell her in my best Han Solo voice if she wants the garbage taken out she should take it out her damned self. She calls me an asshole. I tell her now I am definitely not taking out the garbage and she tells me she wants a divorce. And that, basically, is our marriage. It is, as they say, a lot of hard work.

CHAPTER 14

pills and booze

I feel the need to clarify something lest you get the wrong idea about my life: I am happy. Not all the time, certainly, but happy. More than that, I seem to get happier as the years go by. Not that I don't occasionally think about swerving my car into oncoming traffic, but those sorts of thoughts don't indicate unhappiness. They just mean I'm keeping my options open. Most of the time I'm happy.

Because I'm on pills.

I am a great fan of pills. And while I agree with those who say pills do not solve psychological problems, I am of the opinion that masking the symptoms is just as good as curing the disease.

The "disease" in this case is, of course, depression. I have it. You have it. Everybody has it. Depression is to modern Americans what scurvy was to old-timey sailors, so common it's barely worth discussing. I mention it only insomuch as it affects me, although how much is sometimes hard to tell because even to me, a sufferer, "depression" seems like a fetid load of weaselly claptrap, a cheap and easy excuse for not participating in life.

I do think depression has an evolutionary purpose. Think about it: if your circumstances are miserable enough, you will either do something to change them or die. Our evolutionary trajectory suggests that a lot of us decided to do the former rather than succumb to the latter. That's how we got from fire to the wheel to HDTV.

Plus, if you study history you'll discover that all of history's great minds were miserable fucks. Every single one of them. I know this because I researched every single person who ever lived when writing this book, and the notable ones were all depressed.

Obviously I am not saying that every depressed person is destined for renown, but I *am* saying that if you are a naturally happy person you will never do anything with your life.

This is why all great artists, for example, must be "tortured." Never "upbeat." Never "delightful"; there is no cliché of the "delightful artist." Anyway, who wants to hang around mopey artists in their tattered black clothing, scribbling in their Moleskin journals, smoking their ridiculous organic cigarettes? Even artists want good dental insurance and relationships that do not involve stabbings. But they cannot have these things because they are artists. And artists must suffer.

(Paralegals, as a rule, are not depressed.)

As useful as depression has been in the past, I think it has outlived its evolutionary mandate. When our precarious existence demanded an "innovate or die" mentality, a certain collective ennui made sense. But now that we have frozen pizza and blowjob dolls and everything else we could ever possibly need, depression serves no purpose. It's a vestigial quirk from another time, like the appendix. We don't need it. The only part of society that still benefits from all this misery is the international singer/songwriter cabal. And, of course, the makers of pills.

My antidepressant of choice is Lexapro, the commercial name for a drug called escitalopram. Personally, I prefer the name escitalopram because it is so hard to say. The harder a drug is to pronounce, the more medicinally profound it seems. Lexapro just sounds like a brand of golf ball.

Lexapro belongs to a class of drugs known as selective serotonin reuptake inhibitors (SSRIs), which operate under the same principle as Kevin Costner's urine recycling machine in the movie *Waterworld*. For those not as well versed in *Waterworld* as I, the way it worked is, he peed into a machine, which took out all the toxins, enabling him to drink his own pee. That's what SSRIs do, only with moods.

SSRIs are the most prescribed class of antidepressant in the country, generating tens of billions of dollars in annual global sales. But what's fascinating about them is that doctors don't know if they actually work. Actually "fascinating" might be the wrong word. "Hilarious" is better.

A huge study came out in the *Journal of the American Medical Association* a while ago that basically said researchers could not determine if SSRIs actually do anything to relieve mild depression or not. There is concern, however, that they may *increase* suicidal thoughts and behavior among young people, which is a curious side effect for an antidepressant.

There are a host of other documented side effects including impotence, increased levels of aggression, nausea, urinary retention, weight loss/gain, renal impairment, tinnitus, photosensitivity, and something called "genital anesthesia." (Another way to get genital anesthesia is to rub cocaine all over your dick. Or so I've heard.) Anyway, doctors know SSRIs do all of those things, but they have no idea if they actually treat some of the problems for which they are prescribed.

But they work great for me. Question: how do I know it is actually the drug working and not simply the placebo effect? Answer: I don't. Nor do I care. Whether the drug actually does something or my brain is just gullible does not matter to me at all. Interestingly, another study just came out in the journal *PLoS ONE* (bad name for a medical journal) showing that placebos are still effective *even when the patient knows he is taking a placebo.* In other words, if a doctor gives you a sugar pill and tells you it's a sugar pill, it can still be an effective treatment. So no, I have zero idea whether it's the drug or my brain telling me it's the drug; all I know is that I feel better when I am on my meds than when I am off.

The other thing I've tried recently is booze. I know that alcohol is itself a depressive, but so many people seem to have such a good time with it that after abstaining for my first thirty-five years or so, I thought I should at least give alcohol a try to see if it made my life better and more enriching. The results so far: encouraging.

Kids in my hometown started drinking around seventh grade. Not me. Alcohol scared me. Part of my fear was the belief that any consumption of alcohol at all, no matter how little the amount, would give me bed spins and nausea. I hate nausea. I also believed myself predisposed toward addictive behavior. Once I started drinking, I thought there was a good chance I might never stop. Then I would end up like Edgar Allan Poe. Where this fear originated I do not know. There is no history of alcoholism in my family. (Nor is there any family history of writing Gothic horror stories.) I rarely saw either of my parents drink at all, so perhaps growing up in a dry household made me less likely to take up drinking myself.

Once I made my decision to become a teetotaler, I committed, despite the fact that it seriously affected my ability to endure parties or any social gathering in which alcohol was served, which is to say *every* social gathering. I hated parties. Hated all the slobbery philosophizing and slobbery dancing and slobbery make-out sessions I witnessed. I also found myself having the same boring conversation regarding my drinking again and again:

"Aren't you drinking?"

"No."

"Why not?"

"I just don't drink."

"Did you *ever* drink?" (This is code for: "Are you an alcoholic?")

"No."

"Wow. That's so great, man," they would inevitably say while walking away, drinking.

Of course they walked away. Who wants to hang out with Judgmental Sober Guy? Nobody. Even Judgmental *Drunk* Guy hates Judgmental Sober Guy. Because he feels judged.

And the fact is, I *did* judge everybody around me. My only defense against feeling left out was to feel superior. Looking back, I'm amazed my friends ever invited me to go anywhere at all. Worse, I continue to do it.

This creates problems in my relationship with Martha. She is a moderate drinker, usually consuming about two glasses of wine over the course of a night. Before I started drinking, I found it inconceivable that somebody could drink that much and not be an alcoholic. Yes, I knew the French drink that much, but they are an obviously troubled people. My own ignorance made me worry for Martha, even though she has never shown any symptoms of having a drinking problem. She is simply an aficionado. Martha is to drinking what an enthusiastic bowler is to league night; she can always be counted on to show up and bowl a good game but she is never going to turn pro.

On the rare occasions when she did end up drinking too much, Judgmental Sober Guy was not much help. For example, if she found herself throwing up in the middle of the night, I might help her out by walking into the bathroom, watching her puke for a few minutes, and then saying, "Serves you right," before going back to bed.

The decision to start drinking actually sprang from a desire to improve my relationship with Martha. I know that sounds stupid, but it's true. In an early session with our therapist Suzy, she asked if we had any "rituals," regular activities we enjoy doing together. We couldn't think of any besides watching TV at night, which seemed like the least interesting ritualistic activity imaginable. Earlier in our marriage we had tried playing chess together, but most games ended with me winning and her throwing the pieces across the room and telling me she hated me. Our lack of rituals scared us because Suzy seemed to believe that ritual was a vital component to a healthy marriage. I took it upon myself to begin thinking more seriously about activities we could share. Martha does not enjoy most of the things I enjoy (Scrabble and Ping-Pong) and I do not enjoy what she enjoys (yelling at me). I felt determined to find a ritual. After a while, I did: booze.

I'm fairly confident that wasn't what Suzy had in mind. Furthermore, after consulting the mighty Internet, I discovered a real lack of marriage counselors advising couples to "drink more." But in our case the results have been good.

Cocktail hour begins between five and six each night when the kids have been home from school long enough to make us feel as if we've earned it. That's one good thing about being a parent—children really make you feel as if you deserve your liquor. When they get crazy, as they do in the late afternoon, the only way to get through it is either to tranquilize ourselves or them. For legal reasons, we choose ourselves.

Martha usually initiates the ritual because she is the bigger lush. Several years ago when we were young and pie-eyed about our future, we found ourselves at Crate & Barrel, where we fell in love with and purchased a gunmetal black "apothecary cabinet." At the time, I thought I would use it to display museum-quality objets d'art like Napoleonic era lead soldiers or crystal hippopotamus skulls. But I don't have any museum-quality objets d'art, so we ended up just sticking all our hooch in there.

Typically, Martha fetches a couple of glasses and pours us each a bit of whatever is open. Usually it is wine, but once in a while she makes cocktails. She likes martinis. I like gin and tonics. Drinks in hand, we stand around the kitchen sipping and talking about how annoying the children are.

My early efforts at drinking were not particularly successful. I drank everything too fast because I found the taste so terrible. As a result, I became a gulper, which doesn't look that classy. Wine connoisseurs are unappreciative when you shotgun your 1996 Atlas Peak Cabernet Sauvignon, make a face, and say, "Wow. That really tastes like shit."

Once I learned to slow down, however, I discovered that I could, with some effort, maintain a pleasant equilibrium between mellowness and complete apathy. I think this is what people mean when they say they drink to "take the edge off." It is the pleasant recognition that somebody else is saying or doing something stupid and you don't care. Drinking also makes me feel as if whatever boring thing I have to say is slightly more interesting than it actually is.

After a couple of drinks, I might say to Martha something like "I got a really good score on Boggle today."

"Great," she might reply without even a trace of sarcasm. When that happens, I know the booze has gotten to her, too.

To this day, the only drinks whose taste I actually enjoy are "girl drinks." Anything with ice cream and paper umbrellas is okay by me. When we go out, sometimes I just skip to the back of the drinks menu and order the most effeminate-sounding item they serve.

"I'll have a glass of the house pinot noir," Martha might say.

"And for you, sir?"

"I'll have the Breezy Tampon."

For those wondering if Lexapro and booze are safe to combine, the answer is yes, as long as the alcohol consumption is moderate. If you're wondering if Lexapro and booze *and* Ambien are also safe to combine, there doesn't seem to be as much reliable information on the Internet, and I'm sure it's not recommended by medical experts, but in my personal experience, the answer is also yes.

In addition to the Lexapro and the booze, I have also started taking Ambien. Mostly for fun. I know that sounds terrible, but it's true. Throughout my life, I have rarely had a problem sleeping. In fact, I have the opposite problem. Honestly, I am about a half step away from narcolepsy. Any form of transportation will put me to sleep: train, plane, automobile. I fall asleep on couches, in hammocks, under desks. Yet I take Ambien—not once in a while, but every night.

I am an Ambien addict. Happily so, I might add. I take it because I like it. There is something that happens when I am on Ambien that I find impossible to replicate with regular sleep. I don't know how to describe it except to say I feel as if I am surrendering to a deep and mystifying blackness. It is a dreamless sleep, a sleep without the awareness of sleep, and therefore a sleep without the awareness of self. I love that feeling—the feeling of nothing at all. I call Ambien my "little death," which is also what the French call orgasms because they are, as I said, a troubled people.

This state of selflessness is also what Buddha called Nirvana, although I am sure that he would take issue with my use of Ambien to achieve it but that's only because Buddha didn't have a CVS nearby.

As a person in constant existential dread, maybe it's counterintuitive to ingest something that mimics the annihilation of self. But I find it comforting for some reason. It's like practice death. And if death is anything like Ambien, I have nothing to fear. One minute I'm awake, the next I am obliterated. No muss, no fuss.

I used to think there was something noble about abstention, as if self-denial led to greater clarity of thought or maybe even greater happiness. Turns out, that's bullshit. For me, abstention was about fear: If I am afraid that is usually my signal to pursue something. Walking toward my own fears works for me just as well as pills.

The older I get, the more I allow myself to experience everything out there, and the happier I get as a result. Any new pill that finds its way into my hand will find its way into my mouth. At this point, I'll pretty much try anything. That's neither good nor bad, but it's the truth. Perhaps this is not the most responsible line of thinking for an adult man with two small children, but it works for me. Besides, you have no idea how annoying my kids are.

CHAPTER 15

antivert

Springtime in New York. I'm eating takeout Chinese food at my friend David's apartment. It's my favorite dish: some sort of chicken in some kind of brown sauce.

About half an hour after eating, I stand to leave. As I do, the world starts to go wrong. The wrongness begins as slight dizziness, and then grows in intensity until, within a few seconds, I find I am having trouble remaining upright. I fall back onto the chair, cradling my head in my hands to steady myself. I don't understand what is happening. My first thought is, *Somebody dosed my food.* My second thought, despite my mounting discomfort and panic is, *Awesome.*

David asks me what's wrong. I tell him I'm feeling really weird.

"What kind of weird?" he asks.

"The bad kind," I say.

I feel like I am strapped onto the Rotor, that amusement park ride that spins people around in a giant salad spinner until they are sucked against the wall while pummeling them with dance music. I shut my eyes to eliminate as much visual stimuli as possible. It helps, but not enough. Even with my eyes closed, I can still perceive this awful spinning.

Sitting now is too uncomfortable. I slide from the chair to the floor so that I am flat on my back as the world kaleidoscopes around me. This is awful. Worse, I don't even know what "this" is, although there are only two possible explanations. One is that somebody slipped something into my Chinese food, possibly David, although his motive for doing so is unclear. The only other possible explanation is the one I am inclined to believe: brain tumor.

I have always been remarkably healthy. I almost never get sick, which is a source of great irritation to Martha, who comes down with at least a couple of debilitating colds a year. Although I am obviously fortunate that I do not contract ailments with any frequency, I have always speculated that this might be a bad thing. Perhaps a number of minor afflictions are necessary for the body to purge itself of accumulated toxins. And if the body does not flush these poisons gradually, perhaps over time they will build up until they express themselves in one big fatal blow. As I lie on David's floor, I am convinced that blow has manifested in the form of a (probably inoperable, almost certainly fatal) brain tumor.

David asks if I have any idea how long I'm going to be stuck on the floor like this because he has someplace he needs to go. His utter lack of concern for my well-being is reassuring in a way because it means at least one of us does not think I'm dying. I rub my eyes, trying to get the sensation to clear. I try drinking water. Doesn't help. Several minutes go by. I'm starting to get a little panicky. (I was already panicky. Now I'm getting panickier.)

At no time does David offer to call an ambulance or even his brother-in-law, who is some sort of world-renowned doctor. He doesn't even bother going online to check my symptoms. While I moan on the floor he impatiently flips through TV channels, waiting for whatever is going on with me to resolve itself so that he can get to his next appointment, which I find out later is a squash date. I would like to point out that David is one of my best friends.

Then, as quickly as it started, the sensation stops. Everything just kind of snaps itself into stillness, like a jet fighter landing on the deck of an aircraft carrier. I peek out my eyelids, cautiously sit up, and slowly pivot my head from side to side. When I am satisfied I have regained my equilibrium, I gingerly rise to my feet, keeping a hand rooted to the chair at my side.

"Are you okay?" David asks.

"I think so."

"Are you sure?"

"Yeah, I'm okay."

"Do you think you can leave now?"

My drive home takes more than an hour and I am nervous. Hopefully, if I start to feel ill again, I will have enough time to pull over, but it happened so suddenly and without provocation the first time that there's a good chance I will not have time to get to the side of the road, in which case I will be putting a lot of trust in my air bags.

I arrive home without incident. When I get there, I tell Martha what happened.

"It might be a brain tumor," she says.

I *know* it might be a brain tumor! She's supposed to tell me it's *not* a brain tumor! God, she's annoying!

"It's not a tumor!" I say, before realizing that she has just made me inadvertently spout Arnold Schwarzenegger's catchphrase from the movie *Kindergarten Cop,* which annoys me even more.

She shrugs. I'm not sure if her shrug means, "You're probably right," or "I hope you have our affairs in order." I storm off, pissed. Why does nobody else seem upset that I am dying? Maybe I should tell the kids I'm dying; maybe they will give me more of the terrified reaction I'm looking for.

That night, I can't sleep. There's got to be some reasonable explanation for what happened other than a brain tumor. I just don't think a brain tumor would announce itself so loudly, only to retreat again so quickly. Plus, young men like me don't get brain tumors. I mean, yes, I'm sure young men exactly like me get brain tumors every day, but not young men with my rugged good looks.

Should I see a neurologist? What if I go and he tells me I do, in fact, have a brain tumor? What then? Will they have to do surgery? The only other person I know who underwent brain surgery is my dad, and he died.

The next morning, I feel okay. I putter around the house, monitoring my physical condition. All systems seem go. I even jump up and down a few times to experimentally jar my brain. Nothing. After several hours of careful monitoring, I feel my shoulders descend, my breath deepen. By evening I have recovered enough to feel comfortable bundling yesterday's unpleasantness into a mental box reserved for "unsolved mysteries," something to unpack and wonder over when I am old and not dead from a brain tumor.

Then it happens again. I am by myself upstairs when a sudden whoosh of dizziness throws me to the ground. Within seconds I am flat on my back, nauseated, the heels of my palm pressed against my eyes to blot out any light. I try to stand up, but if I lift myself more than a few inches from the ground, the horizon line tilts and I collapse. I am scared and I need help.

"Martha!" I call.

She's downstairs in the kitchen making dinner and cannot hear me. The kids are down there, too. I'm up here alone. If I want help I'm going to have to go down to get it. Keeping my eyes pressed shut, I crawl across the carpet toward the stairs. Then I hoist myself to my feet, grabbing the banister with both hands to prevent myself from flopping down the stairs like a Slinky. I stumble into the kitchen, falling to the floor on my back. She turns.

"It's happening again," I say.

Emergencies bring out the best in some people. Martha is not one of those people. "What's happening to you?" she says in her outdoor voice. The kids are in the next room playing and I do not want them to panic.

"I'm okay," I say.

"You're not okay! Should I call an ambulance? I'm cooking dinner!"

How much does it cost to ride in an ambulance? It seems to me we should work out the economics here before she makes any rash decisions. Before I can say so, however, she is on the phone with 911. When she hangs up with the emergency operator, she yells at me: "You're going to die and leave me alone with these kids!"

This is not what I want to hear in these, my final moments. I am very sorry that my impending death will be an inconvenience to her, and I am sorry she sees it in those terms. I wonder if soldiers are ever like that in battle? One guy gets shot and instead of reassuring him that he's going to be okay, his buddy says, "You're going to die and I'm going to have to carry all your stuff!"

Several years later on Christmas Eve, our roles are reversed. We are in the kitchen preparing dinner with her friend Yoonsun. Martha is chopping vegetables when she stops suddenly and says, "I just chopped off the tip of my finger."

My first thought is: *Martha is exaggerating because that's what Martha does. There's no way she chopped off the tip of her finger.*

Yoonsun and I look down, and there on the counter is a little piece of Martha's finger. It looks like a little piece of parsnip. In fact, I might have asked if she's sure that it's her finger and not parsnip except for the fact that we're not having parsnips and also because her remaining finger is gushing blood. Yoonsun looks like she might faint.

To her credit, Martha behaves like a trouper. Within moments I have her finger tightly wrapped in paper towels and ice, her fingertip is deposited in a plastic baggie for possible surgical reattachment, and we are out the door, racing to the emergency room. Never at any point do I say to her, "Your hand is going to fall off and I'm going to have to cut your meat for you for the rest of your life!"

Now, as I lie on my back in the kitchen waiting for the ambulance, Martha calls the neighbors, who agree to watch our kids while I die. The kids are still in the living room, oblivious.

Within a few minutes, I hear the ambulance siren, and then the heavy steps of first responders clomping through my home. I allow my eyes to open enough to see a couple of paramedics peering down at me. One of them cannot be older than nineteen and looks like a meth head. I'm concerned he might get a little trigger-happy with the defibrillator.

The other guy looks okay. He's older and has a reassuring mustache. I didn't realize it until that moment, but when it comes to policemen, firefighters, and EMTs, I equate facial hair with competence. The two paramedics regard me the way I might a bird with a broken wing—concerned, but only a little.

"How we doin'?" the one with the mustache asks, in that a-little-too-loud voice people use when they are addressing the old and infirm. His use of the first-person "we" bugs me since *he* is obviously fine and *I* am obviously in the throes of a cerebral meltdown. Plus, what does he expect me to say—fine? Do I look fine?

"Fine," I say.

They've set up a gurney in the hallway, but they can't wheel it to me because it won't fit in our kitchen.

"Can we walk to the gurney?" the mustache asks.

"No," I say. I am immobile. The intensity of the experience has not lessened at all in the fifteen minutes or so since it began. I cannot walk; I do not even trust myself to crawl.

"Okay," the lead paramedic says. "We're going to help you to the gurney."

What I don't realize is that by "help" they mean they are going to grab my arms and literally drag me across the hardwood floor. *This is really embarrassing,* I think, and the embarrassment is nearly as painful as the tumor. I am also concerned with how the kids will react; now that there are actual medical personnel in the house, they have abandoned whatever they were doing to watch. Will they be traumatized to see their father helpless, trawled across the floor like a fishing net? If anything, they think it's funny.

When the EMTs get me to the gurney, they count three, and then lift me up, strap me in, and wheel me through my house toward the front door. I cannot help narrating my journey to myself: *This is the last time I'm going to see this ceiling, the last time I will pass through this door frame, the last time I will go down these steps.*

"Bye!" I call to the kids. "I love you!" These are the last words I will ever speak to them. They do not answer because *SpongeBob* is on.

Outside the air is warm. I scoop it into my chest, knowing it is the last time I will ever breathe fresh spring air. Martha walks me to the ambulance, then follows us to the hospital in her car.

It's my first time riding in an ambulance. Under other

circumstances, I would be excited because my childlike enthusiasm for emergency vehicles has never fully gone away.
The paramedics make small talk with each other during the
trip: the Yankees, the weather, gossip about other paramedics.
Their chatter irritates me because they do not seem to regard
my situation with the gravity that it merits. Occasionally the
senior EMT yells, "We doin' all right?" at me. I give him the
thumbs up. We're doing great.

At the hospital, they wheel me through the emergency
bay and leave me in a small room cluttered with beeping machines. Martha joins me a few minutes later. A no-nonsense
nurse arrives to take my vitals: normal.

After a short wait, the doctor comes in. He's about my age,
which provokes in me an immediate distrust. Doctors should
always be older than me, although he has no mustache, which
is reassuring. EMTs should have mustaches, but not doctors.
He asks a few questions about my medical history. No epi-
lepsy, no head injuries, no neurological problems. After his
battery of questions, it seems to me that he must have ruled
out any mundane explanations for what I have. Therefore it's
got to be something exotic. Probably something he's only read
about it in medical textbooks and never actually seen before.

"I see this all the time," he says.

"You do?"

"Yes. It's very common. You have vertigo."

Vertigo? I didn't think vertigo was a real thing. I thought
it was a made-up movie disease or, at most, a fear of heights
(which is actually called "acrophobia"). And I certainly didn't
think vertigo was "common." How common can something be

if I didn't even think it was real? Does this mean leprechauns are also common?

He tells us that vertigo is usually caused by an inner ear disorder but could be related to a viral infection or migraines or a tumor in the ear or the result of taking certain medications or dehydration or being in an earthquake (after being in an earthquake, survivors often feel the ground moving underneath their feet for days or weeks afterward). In other words, they don't know what causes it.

"Could it be a brain tumor?" asks Martha. I detect a somewhat hopeful tone to her question, not because I think she wants me to have a brain tumor, but because she wants to be right.

"It's possible," says the doctor. "But unlikely."

"So you don't know what causes it?" I ask.

He kind of shrugs. No. He doesn't know. He prescribes a medication called "Antivert," possibly the least cleverly named drug ever. All drugs should have names as straightforward as this one. For herpes: "Antiherp." For chicken pox: "Antichicken."

I take two of the pills and when he checks back in with me about half an hour later, the symptoms have subsided enough that he lets me go home. He reassures me that I shouldn't be worried about vertigo unless it happens again.

"It's already happened twice," I tell him.

"Oh." He considers this. "Well then, if it keeps happening."

The next few days are terrifying. I'm afraid to drive, afraid to move, afraid to do anything that might trigger another episode. If they don't know what causes it, how am I supposed to know how to prevent it? The Antivert doesn't work prophy-lactically, so taking it as a precaution won't do any good. I just have to wait and see if it happens again. Which, of course, it does.

Another attack hits when we are watching TV a few nights later. Even though the doctor has assured me vertigo is no big deal, when it comes, it's just as scary as before. It feels like the planet is trying to throw me overboard. But Martha is now unfazed. "Can you get my Antivert?" I moan from the floor, which I have rolled onto because the couch is no longer hori-zontal enough.

"Can you wait for the commercial?" she asks.

Over the next few weeks, though, the vertigo lessens in frequency and duration, until it disappears altogether. Per-haps I am not dying after all. This is potentially very good news since dying will seriously undermine my efforts to live forever.

I keep the Antivert with me at all times just in case, but after not having any more attacks for a few months, my thoughts about the medication turn from "this could save my life" to "will this get me high?" (Answer: no.)

After a while, it's like the whole thing never happened. Until the following spring, when it happens again. And the spring after that. My best guess is that my vertigo is related to seasonal allergies, which are most pronounced in the spring-time. The allergies probably swell something in my inner ear, which causes the problem. In other words, as unsettling as it is, it's actually no big deal. Vertigo constituted my first legiti-mate adult health scare. Since then, there have been a few others. I have included a short table to inform readers about each.

Symptoms	What I Thought I Had	What I Actually Had
Mickey Mouse–shaped rash across my torso	Scabies	Poison ivy
Lump near my testicles about the size of a gherkin pickle	Testicular cancer	Small hernia
Painful, swollen elbow	Elbow cancer	Bursitis
Blood in my stool	Colon cancer	Beets for dinner

I did have one other health scare when I was much younger, although it wasn't the sort of thing you could take a pill for . . .

CHAPTER 16

fag

Monday morning, tenth grade. I'm changing in the locker room after gym class. Beside me is Dale, a kid I get along with okay. I can't say Dale and I are friends exactly because he's a burnout and I'm a fag, two different categories within our high school's impermeable caste system.

Burnouts can be male or female. They are the kids who take elective automotive repair class instead of geometry. Preferred bands: Led Zeppelin and Pink Floyd. They wear flannel shirts and sneak cigarettes in the bathroom between classes. They bowl. Their hair is long and shaggy. The boys wear work boots and wallet chains. The girls sling tassel-fringed purses on long leather straps. Administratively speaking, burnouts are not "on the college track."

Fags are defined as any guy who does anything creative: if you play an instrument, perform in the school play, draw anything by choice, write anything not assigned to you, or decline to wear acid-washed jeans, you are a fag. Being labeled a fag does not necessarily imply that you are homosexual, just as being Pakistani does not necessarily mean that you're a terrorist. But in certain circles, then as now, one implies the other.

It's New Jersey in the eighties, I'm in high school, and I hate my life.

But Dale's okay. A skinny kid with glasses and thin straw-colored hair, he looks like John Denver crossed with Kermit the Frog. As I said, we're friendly enough, and I don't think twice before turning to him and making the following joke:

"So, Dale, did'ja get laid this weekend?"

It's not a question I would *seriously* ask him. It's not the kind of question I would seriously ask anybody. Also, I already know the answer. Of course he didn't get laid. He's like me, scrawny and unloved. Guys like us don't get to do that stuff. We don't even get to touch boobs yet. That was the point—an acknowledgment that he and I are different from all the hooting bonobo monkeys surrounding us in the locker room, all those hairy, muscular guys slathering themselves in underarm deodorant. Those guys are probably having sex with dozens of girls. Hundreds maybe. In big teenage sex orgies. My question was meant to be a self-deprecating admission of our own sad boyishness among these men.

So I am surprised when he answers, "Yeah."

Yeah? What does he mean "yeah"? That's not the correct answer. The correct answer is "No."

I mean, the answer can't be anything *but* no. There's just no way. Because if Dale is having sex, that means there's no reason *I* shouldn't be having sex, and I am not. I'm better looking than Dale. I'm smarter than Dale. I have an obviously brighter future than Dale. In fact, the only reason I am even friendly with Dale is that I believe myself to be his superior. If he is actually getting it on with somebody then I will have to reevaluate not only my opinion about Dale, but my opinion of myself, an opinion that has already suffered a steady, leaky deflation since puberty began, and which cannot stand to have too much more air taken from it. Therefore, I am forced to conclude that Dale is lying.

"Who is she?" I ask.

"You don't know her." Evasion. He is so full of it.

"I might know her."

"Nah. She lives in Manville."

Manville is the next town over, named for the big Johns Manville plant that used to make asbestos, but which now sits abandoned because people no longer enjoy asbestos.

"What's her name? I know a lot of people there." This isn't true. I don't know anybody who lives in Manville because the only people who live in Manville are burnouts. It is the burnout capital of central New Jersey.

"You don't know her, okay?"

"Maybe I do."

"You don't." His voice pitches up. He's beginning to get mad.

"If I don't know her then what difference will it make if you tell me her name?" He stares at me. I press. "See what I mean? If I don't know her then just tell me her name and I'll let it go. All I'm saying is I know a lot of people in Manville so there's a fairly good chance that I *do* know her."

"Just let it go, okay?" he says.

I am aware that other people are starting to pay attention to our conversation. But I don't care because I know I am on unassailable moral high ground. For some reason, Dale's sexual experiences, real or imagined, have suddenly taken on an outsize importance to my own life, a life that until a few seconds ago had never much considered Dale at all.

But if I can prove Dale to be a liar, or better, if I can humiliate him in front of my peers, perhaps my own social standing will rise. From there it will be only a short step from the bottom rung of the social ladder to the next-to-bottom rung. If I maintain this rate, within a couple of decades I could actually be popular!

So no, I am not going to "let it go," Dale. I will never let it go.

I continue asking for her name, needling him in front of the other guys. Dale grows furious. His shoulders rise up and his head darts from side to side as the other guys come closer. He looks like a mongoose cornered by a snake. He tells me to shut up. But I can't. This attention I'm getting, attention I usually dread, is empowering. I can tell the other guys are enjoying the spectacle, too. They like seeing Dale squirm. I find myself in the unfamiliar role of tormentor and discover to my surprise that I like it. "Is she a ghost? Are you having sex with a ghost, Dale?"

My plan is working. The guys are on my side. They laugh. They like me. These guys are great. Probably they'll want to start hanging out with me. And if they want to hang out, that will mean the girls will be hanging out with us, too. The popular girls, some of whom I bet are on the Pill, which is so awesome it hurts.

Then things start to go bad. Dale stops cooperating with my torment. Instead of accepting my continued ridicule as a gentleman should, he suddenly launches his arms out at me, pushing me in the chest. I stagger backward a step or two. The guys go, "Oooooh."

A physical provocation. I am completely unprepared for this. Oh, dear. The fact that I just thought the words "Oh, dear" should be ample demonstration of just how unprepared I am for things to get violent. Guys about to fight never think, *Oh, dear.* They think, *Bring it on, bitch!*

I'm startled. Why would Dale push me? Doesn't he see how well this is going for me?

He pushes me again. My eyes flick to the gym teacher's office in the center of the room, a glass cage with windows on all four sides like a prison guard's station. It is empty, which is unfortunate. I was hoping our gym teacher was in there because gym teachers really thrive on blowing whistles and breaking things up.

"I told you to LET IT GO!" he shouts at me, pushing me one more time. I am backed up against the lockers now. I hold my palms outward toward him, a peace offering. "Hey c'mon," I say stupidly. "Hey."

Dale is on the balls of his feet, energized. His fists clench and unclench. Somebody starts chanting "Fight. Fight. Fight." Oh dear, oh dear. Somebody else picks it up and in a moment they are all chanting: "Fight! Fight! Fight!"

Shut up! I want to yell at my classmates, my demented bloodthirsty classmates. They should all be in juvy, every single one of them.

Dale's face is flushed, his ratty mongoose head bobbing on the end of his neck. What will I do if he takes a swing at me? My mind quickly devises the optimal strategy: I will fall down. Whether he connects with his punch or not is irrelevant. If I see a fist coming in my direction, I will take a dive. That should stop any further punches, although it does open me up to kicking. I glance down. Yes, he has already changed from his sneakers to his work boots, most likely steel-toed because steel-toed work boots are an important component of the burnout uniform.

He's going to hit me and then kick me and I am going to end up in a wheelchair. But he does not. Instead he says, "Meet me in the parking lot after school," in a tough voice so that he sounds like Fonzie mixed with John Denver crossed with Kermit the Frog.

"Oooooooh!" Mocking laughs all around.

This is terrible. He wants to have a fight. Like, a *fight* fight. Like in those teen movies where kids with pompadours stab each other. I can't fight Dale. I don't know how to fight. I don't know how to throw a punch. I don't even know the right way to make a fist. Thumb inside the knuckles or outside? My only other fight occurred a few years before at our neighborhood bus stop. Eric and I fought a boy for saying something cruel about our sister, Susan. Two against one. He beat us both.

I wish my dad had taught me how to fight before he died, except that I'm pretty sure he didn't know how to fight, either, even though he grew up in Brooklyn and *his* dad was a cop. Why didn't my grandfather teach my dad how to fight so my dad could teach me? What is wrong with the men in my family?

Dale is a burnout and burnouts all know how to fight.

That's what they do. They listen to Led Zeppelin and fix cars and fight, usually with knives, brass knuckles, Chinese throwing stars, and small-caliber guns. They are a savage people. Everybody knows that. Yes, Dale is small and skinny like me, but I have no doubts concerning the outcome of any fight we may have: he will kill me.

What if I refuse? If I back down from a fight, it will be so much worse. These guys already call me names and sometimes give me hard shoves in the hallway for no reason at all, except that I am so easy to displace, gravitationally speaking.

I don't know what to say or do so I just open my mouth and let the truth fall out. "I'm not going to meet you in the parking lot," I say to Dale. I look him dead in the eye, arms at my side.

"Why not?" he barks.

"Because if I do you'll beat me up."

"Pussy!" somebody says. Laughs all around.

He's right. I am a pussy. I am both a pussy and a fag, which seems like an oxymoronic combination, but somehow is not. The momentum has clearly shifted away from me and toward Dale. I can tell I will not be hanging out with the popular guys and their Pill-taking girlfriends anytime soon.

But that's not important right now. What's important is getting out of here without injury. As coolly as I can, I ball up my gym clothes and shove them under my arm. Then I walk past everybody toward the big wooden door that leads from the locker room to the hallway and escape.

"You better be there," Dale calls.

"I won't be there," I call back.

"Faggot!" somebody else says. More laughs.

Although my back is now to the group, I'm pretty sure they've heaved Dale onto their shoulders. They'll probably host a make-out party in his honor with all those popular girls who rightfully should be mine. If Dale didn't have sex before, he definitely will now.

I push on the door and blend into the stream of kids rushing to class. The rest of the day is a terror-filled blur. Spanish. Art. European history. I don't talk to anybody. Lunch: french fries with mustard and a cookie. I see Dale across the cafeteria but I don't think he sees me. I watch him. He laughs with his burnout friends. I assume they are laughing about me. Geometry. English. I make pencil doodles on my desk. I watch the clock. The last bell rings. I spring from my chair, dash to my locker, grab my stuff, and try to get out of there as fast as I can.

The parking lot is a dirt-packed rectangle behind the school where the upperclassmen park their cars. To avoid it, I have to take a different route to exit. Once outside, I half walk, half jog to the convoy of buses idling along the curb. I find my bus and get on and sit somewhere toward the middle, squeezing myself against the window. When it finally fills, the driver closes the hissing door, and we roll past the parking lot, where I see Dale. He stands by himself on a strip of patchy grass facing the school, watching the last trickle of students dribble from the building. As we drive off, I crane my head around, watching him shrink away to nothing.

He confronts me the next day in chemistry. "Where were you?"

My lab partner, Kelly, is pretty and I do not want her to know of my cowardice. She probably knows already. *Everybody* probably knows. I am a teenager and believe people must always be talking about me.

"I told you I wouldn't be there," I say with as much confidence as I can muster, attempting to give off the air of a world-weary man who has seen much and done much and has no need for such foolishness. Does Kelly hear this in my voice? If so, she gives no sign. She never gives any sign of hearing me at all, even though we sit less than two feet away from each other for an entire year.

"Be there today," he says.

"I won't be there," I reply.

After he returns to his desk I blow a scornful little laugh through my nose and, bemused, shake my head at Kelly, as if to say, *Such folly.* But I am invisible to her because I am invisible to girls.

He is waiting for me again in the parking lot after school, but I am tucked safely inside the bus. Our *pas de deux* (French term meaning "one person threatens to beat up the other person, while the other person runs away") continues for a few more days, until he realizes I meant what I said. I am not going to fight him. Once this is clear, he gives up inviting me to get my face punched, and instead just seethes in my direction.

After a few more days I can feel the tension between us ease. Yes, it was an unfortunate turn of events that day in gym class, but such things happen between gentlemen, and I am confident we will soon be back on friendly terms. Or, if not friendly, perhaps we will achieve a cool equanimity.

When I think about it further, I come to believe that Dale is most likely as relieved as me that there is to be no fight. Sure, he was steamed at the time, but deep down, I bet Dale is just as afraid of me as I am of him. Yes I'm on the small side but Dale must have detected a certain wiry toughness in me. In fact, the more I consider the way things unfolded, the more likely it seems that Dale is actually afraid of *me*. After all, if he really wanted to fight, why not just throw a punch in the locker room? Fear. That's why. When viewed in this way, it becomes more and more obvious that the real pussy in this whole matter is Dale.

Unfortunately, this is not how Dale sees it.

On Friday, I am walking back to class after lunch when I suddenly find myself propelled into the cinder-block wall. My books scatter down the hallway. I wheel around, startled and scared. It is, of course, Dale.

"C'mon!" he yells.

Within an instant, a circle of gleeful students has surrounded us. Oh God, we're going to fight. Or rather, he's going to fight and I'm going to be hit. Right here in the hallway where the maximum number of people can see me get my ass kicked.

He lunges again, pinning his head against my chest, driving me backward, swinging at me. I stay on my feet, deflecting his blows but doing nothing to return them. Instead I wrap my arms around him, trying to keep him from hitting me, our sneakers scraping linoleum, the crowd cheering us on. I hear in my head the two words before they are, inevitably, vocalized by some faceless spectator:

"Nerd fight!"

While Dale and I belong to, respectively, the burnout and fag classes of our high school's caste system, when it comes to physical altercations we both fall under the rubric of "nerd," a term that has many meanings, but in this instance means "guys who look stupid fighting."

I fall to the ground and Dale leaps on top of me. Although I am under assault, my main concern now is that my shirt has ridden up, exposing my belly button and possibly my underwear. For some reason, I find this mild indignity far worse than any beating I might suffer.

There is no pain. Dale is not strong. Dale does not know how to land a punch. Dale is a pussy just like me. But Dale is hurting me in ways he does not know, by pointing the hot spotlight of my own inadequacy right in my face. The whole school is seeing me at my most flailing and incompetent. The only thing that could possibly make it worse would be if I started to cry. Which, of course, I do.

The tears come before I can do anything to stop them. They begin as if they are lawn sprinklers set on a timer and do not stop even when two teachers pry us apart and send the crowd scurrying. I am blubbering, choking on my tears. I do not even know why I am crying. Just because, I guess. Because that is what I do when I feel helpless. There is no point in even trying to hide my tears because it's pointless. All of it.

One of the teachers asks me if I am okay. I nod yes because I am currently incapable of speech, unless I want to risk falling into that hiccupy cry-talk little kids do after they've been spanked.

The teachers have us each hooked at the elbow. I know what's next: quick march down to the office, interrogation, suspension. My mom will kill me. The only upside to being suspended will be staying home by myself for a few days, even though Mom will undoubtedly give me a lengthy list of chores to fill my time. That's what she did the time I forged her signature and then said, "Heil, Hitler" to her when she grounded me. (Turns out parents, particularly Jewish parents, do not like being compared to Hitler.)

This will be worse, though. Suspension is just a step away from expulsion. Expulsion is just a step away from homelessness. Which is just a step away from blowing dudes at the bus station for a slice of pizza.

But the teachers do not take us to the office. Instead they make Dale and me shake hands. When we do, I can see in his eyes that we're even now. He feels victorious and I am almost happy for him to feel that way. I almost say, "Nice job," but I feel like it will be interpreted sarcastically, and besides, I cannot speak.

The class bell rang a long time ago. When the teachers are satisfied we are done making violence, they send us to our classes. Me to AP lit, Dale to auto shop or wood shop or whatever vocational class he is taking to prepare himself for the world. After collecting my fallen books, I take a detour into the boys' room to inspect myself. I am undamaged. Just kind of snotted up. I wash my face and lock myself in a toilet stall.

While sitting there, I try to cheer myself up. It's over. I survived. Dale got his revenge and the natural order has been restored. Yes, people will probably make fun of me a little

more than usual for the next week or so, but then they'll forget about it. As far as humiliations go, getting beat up is pretty
run-of-the-mill. Certainly not as bad as getting caught jerking
off in class like Sam Dewar. The girl behind him in Algebra II
caught him doing it behind his textbook and screamed. Sam
had to move to an entirely different town after that.

Lucky him.

CHAPTER 17

i am a demographic

Even though I used to look down on kids like Dale who took auto repair class, a huge part of me is pissed off at myself that I never bothered to learn anything about cars, since even from a young age, I admired fast-moving shiny things: rockets, trains, airplanes, cars. Especially cars. But I never bothered to learn anything about how they work, which is embarrassing. I mean, guys are expected to know *something* about cars; at the very least, a man should be capable of changing a tire. I cannot. All I know is that the process involves something called "lug nuts," a piece of information I have retained because "lug nuts" is a funny thing to say.

Nor do I know how to change the oil. I'm not even sure how to properly *check* the oil, although it too involves a funny word: *dipstick*. Honestly, I am so incompetent when it comes to cars I do not trust myself to tie a Christmas tree to the roof. I rely on Martha to do that because she is a Christian.

But as I said, I like cars, and have always admired men who understand them. To me, there is no greater attainment a man can reach than to be able to look under the hood of a car and diagnose a busted fan belt. How I would love to say those words one time with a straight face: "You've got yourself a busted fan belt." Or "Looks like you've got a crack in your thingy." (See? I couldn't even think of another appropriate engine component so I had to go with "thingy.") How I would love to even know where the latch is to open the hood.

My own car is a gunmetal gray 2007 BMW 328xi, and it's the fanciest thing I have ever bought myself. Like most other actions I undertake, its purchase was accompanied by a sense of terrible shame.

The first and most obvious reason for my shame was the financial indulgence. How could I possibly justify spending forty-two thousand dollars on a car when I had not yet saved enough money for my children's college education?

I could not.

Did that stop me? It did not.

The second, deeper level of shame had to do with my own sense of self. I just never envisioned myself being the kind of guy who would drive a car like that. Because there *is* a type of guy who drives an expensive, finely tuned Bavarian automobile. That type of guy is commonly referred to as a "douchebag."

When I am growing up in my crummy town house in my crummy New Jersey town, there is a bright young family who lives next door. The family is headed by an eager middle-manager-looking guy named Bill. He's got a beautiful brunette wife and two beautiful, popular daughters who have straight white teeth perfected by years of pricey orthodontia.

Sometimes in the morning I see Bill leaving for work. He always wears a suit and he's got the same crispy, swept-back hairstyle as the local news anchor. From our upstairs bedroom window, I watch him trot out of his house, his tan leather briefcase dangling from his arm like a magician's assistant.

Where he goes, what he does, I don't know. I imagine he's got "clients" and "accounts." He probably has a secretary, and he probably says to her, "Get my clients on the phone! I need to speak to them about their accounts!"

They are probably screwing while he says this.

At around six each night, he returns to his house and all his winsome girls. I imagine them in their snug home eating a fine meal. I imagine our family is a frequent topic of conversation, and when they talk about us, I imagine them laughing and laughing and laughing.

For years, I watch Bill's comings and goings, and every time I think to myself, *That guy is a douchebag.* His car of choice: a BMW.

The car represents an aspirational lifestyle to which I do not aspire. I do not want to be like all the world's Bills and Chets and Rogers, guys with meaty handshakes and office football pools. Not that there's anything wrong with guys like that. It's just that they are all, as I said, douchebags.

The life I envision for myself does not hold fancy cars. When I think of my own future, I imagine I will be like one of the kids from the movie *Fame,* a perpetually teenage artist singing and dancing on high school cafeteria tables and the roofs of New York City taxicabs.

I will be pure, untouched by the feverish demands of corporate America. Yes, I will be poor, but happily so. My friends will all be artists of one kind or another: modern dancers and sculptors and jazz pianists, and probably some of them will overdose on heroin or jump off bridges. It will all be so tragic that the rest of us will not know what to do, so we will console each other with sex.

I will spend my days sitting on the windowsill of my tiny bohemian apartment writing long poems, which will be beautiful, yes, but also hypermasculine. They will have metaphoric titles like "Tribeca Slaughterhouse, 3 a.m." I will never show these poems to anybody, yet they will somehow become world-famous.

In a world unbound by society's rules, there will be no place for fancy cars. Because everybody knows that fancy cars are for guys like Bill. Sellouts. Dopes. Squares.

So a couple of decades later, when I find myself walking into the gleaming BMW dealership, my own beautiful wife and kids in tow, I find myself looking over my shoulder. For what, I am not sure. Possibly my younger self giving me the finger.

Compounding my shame is the fact that I already own two perfectly good cars. Yes, they are getting old, but both remain operable. The first is a hulking Jeep Grand Cherokee that we bought before people cared about the earth. The second is my Volkswagen New Beetle, purchased because Martha thought it was cute. Originally the car was hers, but now that we have two kids, it has become mine. I have never felt as defensive about a possession as I do about that Beetle.

"It's not a girl's car," I tell people. They don't even have to suggest otherwise for me to tell them this. I say it reflexively.

Sometimes I say it when giving my order at the McDonald's drive-thru.

"Can I take your order?"

"It's not a girl's car."

But it *is* a girl's car. Moreover, it is a *young* girl's car. It is the Justin Bieber of automobiles. It's like driving around in a copy of *Seventeen* magazine. When you honk the horn, it squeals. It's simply not an appropriate vehicle for a fully grown, ruggedly handsome man such as myself. The car is nothing more than a smooth round bump; it looks like a shaved vagina.

I spend five years driving that car. Five years of slouching down in my seat while idling at stoplights beside attractive women in Porsches or Jags. Finally I cannot take it anymore. I need a sexier car, a man's car. I need a BMW.

Wandering around the showroom, I feel like a fraud. I mean, I'm obviously not the kind of guy who hangs out in BMW showrooms. I'm obviously nothing like the other thirty-something white guys here with *their* families, all of them pretty much dressed exactly like me. Those other guys, they're everything I'm not. Just look at them, with their . . . shoes?

I admit, it may not be easy to differentiate us based on appearances. But I need to hold on to the idea that I am not *exactly* like these other guys. I need to believe that I fall outside the boundaries of some market-tested demographic. This idea, that I am somehow *different,* is central to my entire sense of who I am. Yet here I am wandering around what appears to be a gathering place for people who are exactly like me. All of us the same. The only consolation I have is that we are all pretty good-looking.

Worse, if I squint, we could all be my neighbor Bill twenty-five years ago.

I need to get out of here.

"Can I help you?" A saleswoman is at my side. She does not seem to care that I have just come to the earth-shattering realization that I am a demographic.

Can she help me? I don't know. What can she do for panic attacks?

I mention to her that I might, possibly, be interested in a car. Do I have a specific model in mind? I shrug. Perhaps, maybe, the newly redesigned 328 six-cylinder all-wheel drive coupe that *Car and Driver* magazine just called "Best in Class"? Maybe that one? Not that I've spent every night for the last two months online researching it or anything.

"Of course," she says, leading me to a sparkly model on the showroom floor. We stand beside it and I nod as she spends the next ten minutes discussing weight distribution and gear throws and the new ventilated all-disc brakes. Uh-huh. I have no idea what she is talking about. Mostly I just want to lick it.

As stupid as I feel listening to her blather on, I am keen on not *appearing* stupid. So I assume my wide Car Guy stance. Feet shoulder width apart, arms folded over each other, face set into a concentrated grimace. This is the position I take when people talk to me about things that guys are supposed to know about: cars, football, fishing, any kind of mechanical system. I want her thinking to herself, *From the way he is nodding and standing with his feet shoulder width apart, I can tell this guy really knows his shit.*

To her credit, she is not condescending and never gives

any indication that she is onto my ruse. Or maybe my Car Guy performance worked. I bet it did. Especially the part after she showed me the engine and I said, "She's a beaut."

At the end of her spiel she asks if I'd like to take a test drive.

Yes I would.

She returns with the key. When I look around for a place to insert it, she tells me there is no keyhole. All I have to do is push a button on the dashboard labeled "Start," just like the Batmobile. Cool. Does this car make me appear more like a superhero? I think perhaps it does. I look for a button labeled "Missiles" but find none.

I start her up and drive the family around for a few miles. The ride is enjoyable, spoiled only by Martha and me screaming "DON'T TOUCH ANYTHING!" at the kids every ten seconds. They touch everything. Before we have pulled out of the parking lot the backseat windows are streaked with greasy kid-size palm prints. This is *exactly* why the Batmobile is a two-seater.

Martha asks how it drives.

"Very responsive," I say. "Taut."

What? Did I just say "taut"? I did. God, I hate myself. At a stoplight we switch positions so she can have a turn driving it, too. She stalls it out when the light turns green. Women.

When we get back to the dealership the saleswoman asks me what I think. I return to my Car Guy stance, murmuring something noncommittal. I tell her I'll think about it and get back to her. But there's no question in my mind: I am buying that car. How do I reconcile my conflicting emotions about the automobile? That's easy: in any conflict between idealism and shininess, shininess wins.

Deciding to buy the car is like getting into a hot bath after deliberately subjecting myself to the cold for as long as I could stand it. For years, I have identified myself as somebody who lives outside the demands of commerce; I *became* that perpetually teenage artist dancing on taxicab roofs. But what I never realized until this moment is that, not only am I currently a demographic, I always was one. The iconoclast is as well defined a demographic as the yuppie and the soccer mom and the redneck. We are *all* demographics. Even guys like me who do everything in our power to self-identify as "different"; in fact, the BMW 328xi is specifically marketed to people who think of themselves in *exactly this way.*

Marketers have thought of everything. They knew I would want this car before I even knew. Which is to say, they know me better than I know myself. Some people might find that creepy. I find it comforting. Because not only do they know me, they *like* me. They like all of us here in the BMW showroom, all of us craving the aggressive, masculine, deeply meaningful lifestyle embodied by these handsome automobiles with their taut steering. They know us because their only mission in life is to satisfy these deep American cravings that resonate across the vastness of our culture like whale songs.

They are the people who create the itch and scratch of American life. And as much as I resisted it, I have to admit there was something kind of wonderful about succumbing to the temptation, of buying admittance to a club whose badge is the blue and white propeller hood ornament on our delicious Bavarian automobiles.

I'm not being hyperbolic here, either. Such societies literally exist. There are BMW car clubs all over the country. Look at this quote from the home page of the BMW Car Club of America:

> You know that little flash of camaraderie that washes over you when you see a pair of BMW kidneys coming down the road? If you even know what that question means, you're either already a member, or should be. You have to own a BMW to understand.

I love that phrase: "You're either a member, or should be." That's exactly right. I *should* know that little flash of camaraderie, that wink of recognition between men like me: successful men, powerful men, men who kite-surf. No, I am not one of these men, but I *should* be. That is the wink, a wink that says: *You and I know secrets that drivers of lesser cars will never know.* I am not yet a member of this society, but I will be. All I have to do is press "Start."

Back home, I call every BMW dealer within a fifty-mile radius to ask for their best deal. I tell them exactly how I want my new Beemer tricked out. Yes, I want heated seats and GPS. No, I don't want the sport package because the online forums tell me it's a rip-off, even for kite-surfers such as my future self. No, I don't want Steptronic paddle shifters. All my shifting will be done the way God intended transmissions to be shifted, by hand.

After a dozen calls, I manage to get the price knocked down a few thousand dollars. Unfortunately, the best quote I get does not come from the place where I took the test drive. I feel bad about that because I liked the woman who helped me out, but I figure BMW salespeople are probably used to dealing with upwardly mobile businessmen such as myself so she understands that with guys like us, the dollar is king. It's just business, baby.

I order my car. They tell me two months. To make the long wait for the car more tolerable, BMW has thoughtfully created a website where I can check the progress of my car from its assemblage by wood nymphs in the Bavarian forests, to its transatlantic voyage on the *QE2*, through its final transport to my dealership borne on the wings of angels.

Two months later, as promised, it arrives. Martha drives me to the dealership to pick it up.

"I'll meet you at home," she says.

Yes, good. Let us meet at home sometime in the future. Right now, I need some alone time with the car. I spend the first twenty minutes of our time together just admiring how good I look in it. My God, I am handsome in this car. I look very good in the rearview mirror, both side mirrors, and in the reflection I catch of myself through the windshield when I angle my head just so. If I tilt the electric heated seat all the way back, I see that I also look good in the sunroof. Picture a cowboy riding a bucking great white shark. That's pretty much how I look.

On the drive home, I dawdle at stoplights, waiting for panties to be thrown at me through my open window. I rev the engine and crank the radio full volume. ("Full volume" for me means a little bit louder than background music because I have sensitive ears—also, I should note that I am listening to NPR.) I career through narrow turns on the country roads near my home at speeds marginally higher than the posted speed limit. I am James Dean.

I love my new car. I park it in conspicuous places. I go to the car wash all the time. One time I buy *and use* an aerosol can of hubcap cleaner. When driving, I derive immense satisfaction from shifting into sixth gear, a gear unknown to my Beetle. I call it my "Fuck the police" gear.

With time, however, my excitement over the new car diminishes. The kids inject irretrievable food morsels into the rear seat folds, the creamy leather becomes stained from my blue jeans, the fuel consumption is a bit on the greedy side, I stop using sixth gear after a speeding ticket, and when I pass another BMW on the road, I do not feel that promised wink of camaraderie. Honestly, there are very few winks at all because I feel stupid winking at other guys.

I do not join the BMW Car Club of America.

Several thousand miles later, however, something wonderful happens. It's a small thing. While I am driving one day, the built-in video monitor on my dashboard informs me the oil needs to be changed. I like the way it tells me this: "The oil needs to be changed," not "*You* need to change the oil." The distinction is subtle but important. The car knows I am incapable of changing the oil myself and does not judge me for it.

Car Guys used to accomplish such tasks themselves. When I was younger, I used to see them out on their driveways with assorted screwdrivers and drip pans. Every man was expected to know how to perform this little bit of mechanical alchemy. Needless to say, I never learned nor had any desire to learn. Now, though, my BMW's oil tank (chamber? holder? cup?) is located in a spot inaccessible to mere mortals. It requires the steady hand of a certified professional. Or maybe a robot. Maybe even a certified professional robot.

Regardless, the car lets me know that it's okay, preferable even, that I bring it into the shop. It's okay that I don't understand its inner workings. I don't understand my wife's fallopian tubes, either, yet we still managed to make two children just as beautiful as my old neighbor Bill's daughters from so long ago. Even better, *my* kids don't need braces. Their teeth are naturally perfect. So you can just go ahead and suck it, Bill.

My BMW loves me despite my ignorance. It does not care that I'm a flawed driver, that I often take turns too wide and occasionally stall out on steep hills when my foot and hand do not cooperate in the "ol' clutch-n-shift," which sounds like a euphemism for masturbation but is not.

The car likes me for who I am. Just a guy pretty much like millions of other guys. In fact, she tells me how much she likes me each time I push her little clitoral start button. Not with words, but with the smooth purr of her engine. *You are just like everybody else,* she tells me as we glide down the interstate, *just like everybody else . . .*

I find the thought oddly comforting. After years of fighting to distinguish myself, the idea that I don't have to be unique feels as cozy to me as a blanket just out of the dryer. I don't need to be different, don't need to be better. The aspirational lifestyle turned out to be a lifestyle in which I am just another middle-aged dude, and I have to say, there are times when being just another middle-aged dude is fine by me. Yes BMW, we are all the same. Me, you, my old neighbor Bill, Dale, FKF, everybody. All of us speeding toward the same destinations, singing along to the same old songs on the radio, tumbling the same quiet thoughts over and over in our minds. None of us better than the other. All of us the same. Except that I have a nicer car.

CHAPTER 18

nibbles

A recent conversation in our house:

Martha says, "I want a cat."

I say, "I don't want a cat."

Martha says, "The kids want a cat."

"We want a cat!" the kids say.

"*I* do not want a cat," I repeat, emphasizing the word *I* and utilizing my "royal decree" voice, a tone I reserve for those times when, as household patriarch, I exercise my right to end the conversation. The conversation does not end.

"But cats are cute," says Martha.

"So are chimpanzees," I say. "Are you also saying we should get a chimpanzee?"

"We want a chimpanzee!" say the kids.

A twenty-minute discussion follows about why we are not getting a chimpanzee. The matter of the cat, however, is still up for discussion.

I have nothing against cats per se. I just don't want to add to the long list of living creatures already under my care. I am responsible for the well-being of several human beings, including a couple of kids in Bangladesh I send money to every month because Save the Children made me feel guilty. Plus, we have our dog, Lily, who is sweet and getting old and probably does not want some cat sleeping in her chair. Adding a cat to the mix would just gum up the works for everybody.

Also, I do not want to clean a litter box.

"You won't have to," Martha says. "I'll do it."

She is a liar.

I know she is a liar because she said the same thing the last time we brought a new pet home.

At age seven, Elijah announces that he wants a hamster. Everybody seems to think this is a terrific idea, except me, for all the same reasons I do not want a cat: extra work, I will not love it, etc. Plus, I suspect it will come to a bad end since small rodents tend not to live very long. When I was five, I awoke one morning to find my own guinea pig, Mork, lying on his side at the bottom of his cage, stiff as fiberboard. The same thing will happen with a hamster, inflicting unnecessary trauma on our young children.

This argument, like every argument I have ever made to my wife, fails.

I take Elijah to the local pet shop to buy a hamster. The selection is somewhat limited. They have two. One is brown with white. One is white with brown. We decide on the more brownish one because he seems spunkier. (We call the hamster "he" because we do not know how to determine the hamster's gender, so I allow Elijah to assign it one.) Elijah already has the hamster's name picked out: Nibbles, which I have to admit is a solid choice.

On our way out of the pet shop, I quietly ask the woman how long hamsters live.

"About three years," she says.

Nibbles takes up residence at the top of Elijah's dresser. He is a good hamster and seems to enjoy doing all the classic hamster things: running on his wheel, clambering through a plastic Habitrail, burrowing through cedar shavings, and of course, nibbling. One habit he has that would be amusing if it didn't seem so desperate is clinging to the top of his aquarium by his teeth, clawing and chewing at the plastic liner, his little legs dangling in midair, until his body weight finally drags him back to the cage bottom, where he shakes himself off and then does it again. It is unclear to me whether this is an enjoyable diversion for him or if, like a Haitian boat person, he is willing to risk his life for freedom.

Elijah is a surprisingly good pet owner, often taking Nibbles out of his cage to play, putting him in the little plastic hamster ball we bought, or sometimes closing the bedroom door and just letting the hamster roam free. Elijah is a much better pet owner than I was at his age. I never played with Mork at all. Poor Mork.

Once a week or so, Nibbles's cage needs to be cleaned. Elijah does his best to help, but aside from being an enthusiastic sprayer of Windex, he is useless. Which means that either Martha or I needs to do the hard work of dumping the moist wood liner into the garbage and scrubbing poo pellets from the corners. It's an annoying, smelly process that takes about half an hour. Not a big deal, but Martha promised me she would do it. That was the deal before I agreed to get the hamster in the first place. I remind her of her promise.

"I never said that," she says.

"Yes you did," I respond.

"If I did, I don't remember."

It is a devastatingly effective response. I seem to remember Ronald Reagan saying something similar regarding the Iran-Contra scandal, and that guy is a goddamned American hero.

So there I am, week after week, hauling garbage bags filled with urine-soaked wood chips to the trash. Each time I do, I seethe with resentment at my lying wife. This goes on for eight months. Then Nibbles dies.

The kids are devastated, but Martha and I have been through this before. We had another dog before Lily, another yellow-white lab named Mattie. This was before kids, before marriage, when Martha and I were just trying out our roles as capable, loving adults. I'd been thinking about getting a dog for a long while, even before Martha moved in with me. I don't know why. Companionship, I guess, and a lack of understanding of what a pain in the ass owning a dog in New York City would be.

In warm weather, animal rescue agencies set up adoption centers all over the city. I often found myself stopping to look at the dogs, feeling a peculiar heart tug, an emotion hovering halfway between longing and dread. After a while, I would tear myself away and continue about my day. This went on for more than a year.

But I couldn't quite bring myself to pull the trigger and

actually take one home. Wouldn't it be too much work? What if I wanted to leave town for a week or two? I had many valid reasons not to bring home an animal. And yet, I kind of wanted a dog.

After Martha moved in with me, she encouraged me to adopt. Confronted with all of my reasons for not getting one, she responded with pretty straightforward logic about why I should: "If you want a dog, you should get a dog." Outwitted again.

So one Saturday morning in the spring, we take the subway uptown to an animal shelter. Martha and I are both adamant that we should adopt a shelter dog. It feels like the morally correct thing to do, allowing me to play Oskar Schindler for a day.

When we arrive at the shelter, we are greeted by an affable young woman who has me fill out some forms and asks me a series of questions about my ability to care for a pet. Then she gets a little more personal: how much do I make? I give her an approximate figure. She asks to see a bank statement. I do not have a bank statement. It never occurred to me to bring a bank statement to the animal shelter because I did not think income verification would be part of the pet adoption process. For a human child perhaps, but not for an animal that would otherwise be put to death. I do happen to have an ATM statement crumpled in my pocket, which shows my current checking account balance. (Not to brag, but it is considerable. Okay, I am bragging.) I show it to the lady thinking, *Surely, this will suffice.*

It does not suffice.

"I'm sorry," she says.

"But this shows how much money I have."

"It's not a bank statement."

"Yes, but it's a statement from a bank."

"But it may not be *your* statement from *your* bank."

I show her that the last few numbers on my ATM card match the last few numbers on the statement. I offer to go to an ATM and procure another, identical statement. She can even come with me if she wants to make sure no pet adoption chicanery is taking place. No. Only an official bank statement will do. Is she kidding?

She is not kidding.

She tells me to come back when I have a proper bank statement. But I do not want to come back. Coming back means waiting until Monday, when my bank is open. I don't want to wait. I don't want a dog on Monday. I want a dog NOW! Surely, even Oskar Schindler never had to work as hard as this!

We leave, incensed. Fuck those shelter dogs. Let them die.

My only recourse is to find a pet store. Any pet store will do. I will march into the first one I find and bellow, "Show me your dogs!" I will select their most expensive specimen, fit it with a rhinestone-crusted collar, and buy every single stupid squeaky toy they have. Then I will march back to the animal shelter, where I will press my new dog's face against the window and scream, "LOOK AT MY EXPENSIVE DOG!" to the hard-hearted woman within. Then I will run away.

Martha is with me up to the part about going to a pet store. After that, she tells me, I am on my own.

As it happens, there is a pet store only a few blocks from the shelter. It's one of those mom-and-pop places that smell like wood shavings and pee. Lined against one wall are dozens of small cages, each holding a newly born pup. The dogs lie on their tummies or chew on their cage doors or wrestle in ripped-up newspaper. The whole thing is so cute I feel my glands shrivel to prevent adorable overdose.

Toward the rear of the store is the dog that will become our dog. She is fat and white, and comes wagging up to me when I kneel down in front of her. She pokes her wet black nose through the squares of her cage door.

"Can we see this one?" I ask a salesgirl.

The girl takes us to a special area in the back where they introduce dogs to prospective buyers. It is quieter back here, away from children and birds and the jangling bell that rings whenever the front door opens.

Freed from her cage, the dog seems shy and unsure of herself. I bend down to her, hold out my hand. After a few tentative moments, she waddles over and sniffs me. I stroke her head and rub her pink tummy.

"What do you think?" I ask Martha.

"She's really cute."

"You wanna come home with us?" I ask the dog.

"Yes," says the dog. "I would like that very much." (It's hard to tell if the voice I hear is the dog's or my own, speaking in a darling, puppyish falsetto.)

And just like that, we have a dog.

We call her Mattie. I will spare you all the enchanting dog moments we share with her because the only thing worse than hearing parents talk about their babies is hearing "parents" talk about their pets. Suffice to say, we love her. We hate her, too, because she needs to be walked and bathed and cared for like an actual living creature.

Martha and I have many early morning fights about whose turn it is to take out the dog, fights that foreshadow the ones we will have with Elijah in just a few years. Despite lessons, Mattie never learns to walk well on a leash. She pulls, gets tangled up, leaps at other dogs, squirrels, pigeons. She happily ignores oncoming traffic and chokes herself hoarse trying to lick puked-up beer from the gutter. My Baggie-wrapped hand becomes intimately familiar with the shape and texture of her poo, so much so that I grow immune to any disgust I would normally feel when handling fresh-baked feces. This is a skill that will serve me well later when I have diapers to change and asses other than my own to wipe.

Very quickly, she becomes the best part of our life together.

A couple of years later, we are living in Los Angeles. Mattie is full-grown but retains her enthusiasm for indoor barking and throwing herself on every single person who walks through our door. As a result, all of our friends hate Mattie. One friend in particular makes a point of saying so—subtly—whenever he visits.

"I hate your dog," Will tells me each time he comes over.

Even so, when Martha and I have to go out of town for a couple of weeks, Will agrees to watch Mattie. Now that I am a parent of actual humans, I can't imagine asking somebody who hated my kids to babysit, but that's pretty much what we did with Will. At the time, Will needed a place to stay, so the arrangement made sense for all parties. "Needs a place to stay" is not a good qualification for a babysitter any more than "I don't want to be an old mom" is a good reason to have kids, but whatever.

When we return from our trip, Will and Mattie seem to have reached détente. The only problem, Will tells us, is that Mattie has not been eating much.

"Is that because you haven't been feeding her?"

Will insists he was not trying to starve the dog in our absence. She just didn't seem hungry. This is a worrisome development, and after observing her lack of appetite ourselves, we schedule a visit to the veterinarian.

It takes a few days and some X-rays to get the diagnosis. Our two-and-a-half-year-old dog has cancer. We're both stunned. How could she have cancer? The vet tells us it's not that uncommon, particularly among Labs, and particularly among puppy farm Labs, the kind you might buy at a New York City pet store, say.

The tumors are spread throughout her torso, too many to consider surgery, leaving us with two options: either we try to treat her, or we don't. If we don't, of course, she will die. And if we *do* treat her she still might die. Just like with people, cancer treatments for dogs are very expensive and not necessarily effective. The doctor tells us up front that the odds of saving her aren't very good, but we don't feel like we have an alternative. She is our dog and we will do whatever we can and spend whatever money it takes.

Soon Mattie is on a regular chemotherapy schedule. We drive an hour each way to the clinic, where her leg is shaved and she is injected with a scary red liquid that leaves her sluggish and sick, so sick in fact that, when she pukes, she does not even bother licking up her own vomit like the old Mattie would. Old Mattie loved the taste of her own sick.

Mattie has always been terrible in the car, pacing and howling, but generally excited to go wherever we happen to be going. Now she is afraid to even get in the car because she knows where we are going, and she knows it's going to hurt. As upset as she is by these trips, she never growls or snaps or seems to blame us for what is happening to her.

After a couple of months, her tumors shrink. Her appetite returns, she regains her energy, and we grow optimistic. Maybe the treatment worked. Maybe the cancer was like an aggressive but shallow-rooted weed that just needed a good course of pesticide. But no. The cancer returns, worse than before, and the drugs seem to lose their potency. Soon the vet is telling us we've exhausted our treatment options. He tells us Mattie is going to die.

The next few weeks are agonizing. Mattie lies around, unwilling to do much more than shift from one uncomfortable position to another. Some friends come over to play cards one night. She does not greet people at the door as she used to. Instead she spends the night under the card table, her head resting on my foot. Even Will is sweet to her when he leaves that night. He pats her on the head and says goodbye.

One day, she seems to feel a little bit more like herself, so we put her back in the car for a ride, driving up the coast to a small public beach in Malibu. We ignore a sign that reads: "All dogs must be on leash," and spend a few hours throwing a tennis ball for Mattie, who chases it into the water and brings it back to me to throw again.

A few days after that she can't breathe without a struggle. We call the vet. He tells us she is in pain. He listens to our description and then advises us to put her to sleep. Can we wait? Yes, but her symptoms will not improve. Her pain will only worsen. He can't tell us what to do, he says, but if it were his pet, he would do it now. We should bring her in. No, we say, we want her to die at home. Does he know any good vets who come to your house to kill your pet? He gives us a number to call.

A small, quiet man arrives at our house a few hours later carrying a black leather satchel just like doctors in old movies. He walks to Mattie, who lies in the living room, her breath heavy. When he calls her name, her head lifts and she raises herself from the floor, tail wagging. He murmurs to her. Martha and I exchange hopeful looks. Maybe we don't have to do this now. He rubs his hands against her flanks, presses a stethoscope against her side. Looks in her eyes. He tells us he thinks it's time.

The vet gives us a few moments to talk, then asks what we want to do. We look at each other and I tell him okay. At least some of the reason I have just agreed to let him kill my dog is that I feel bad he drove all the way out here.

"Let's do it in the bedroom, on her dog bed."

He says that's fine.

225

I ask if I can be in there with her.

Yes.

Martha says she can't watch.

I don't know if I can watch, either, but I want the last face she sees to be one of ours. The three of us go into the bedroom. Mattie curls up on her bed, tail still thumping. I sit on the floor beside her while the doctor extracts his vials and syringe.

I scratch behind Mattie's ears and tell her I love her. I go "shhh," over and over even though she's not making any noise. The doctor inserts the needle into her side. Mattie flinches a little at the needle prick, but after a few seconds starts to relax as the first drug, a sedative, takes hold. I feel my chest seizing up. "Shhh," I say to her and I am crying. "Shhh." Her eyes start to glaze over, but she is still here. I know she's still here, I can see her watching me. Her eyes are deep and clear and she is dying. I can't sit here. I can't. Before I know what I'm even doing, I am on my feet and fleeing the room. Leaving Mattie before it is done is the single greatest shame of my life.

Martha stands, arms crossed over her chest, in the living room.

"Is it over?"

I can only shake my head no.

A few minutes later the doctor emerges from our bedroom, his black bag zipped tight. I write him a check, thank him, and he leaves.

*   *   *

Twelve years later, Nibbles dies in his cage. It's not a surprise. He'd been fading for days: his eyes were closed, his annoying nocturnal wheel-running had ceased, and he suddenly looked old. Yes, a hamster can look old. They get kind of gray around the muzzle and they start asking you to speak up.

It was obvious to us that Nibbles was on his way out. Martha tried to prepare Elijah for the inevitable, but to no avail. He kept saying things like "I don't want to think about it," which I believe is the correct way to approach any problem. Denial. He also retained a certain amount of optimism about the situation. His diagnosis: "Maybe Nibbles is tired." Indeed. Tired of life, boy. Tired of life.

We had no way of determining Nibbles's age. The lady at the pet shop told me hamsters live to be three. We'd only had Nibbles in our lives for eight months, but it's possible he was geriatric before we even got him. We didn't know his age. We didn't know his gender. Nibbles, there was so much about you we didn't know.

When Nibbles finally succumbed, Elijah at first said he was okay with it, and did not miss Nibbles very much. (Step One of the Five Stages of Death, according to Elisabeth Kübler-Ross, of course, is Denial.) Next came the tears. Elijah started crying, which made Ruthie cry. Soon they were both keening over the dead hamster. Mourning in the free and un-self-conscious way that children cry, their tears feeding other tears, followed by desperate exhortations to the gods: "Why?" my son asked. "Why?" (Step Two: Anger.) He was choked up and tearful, which was both very sad and very cute. (Step Four: Depression.) After Martha suggested he eat dinner in front of the television, a never-before-granted privilege, he cheered up immediately. (Step Five: Acceptance.) It should be noted he skipped over Step Three: Bargaining, in which the bereaved attempts to bargain with God. I guess he didn't think of it.

We bury Nibbles in the backyard, right at the edge of the woods. He will be returned to the earth, a boy's beloved pet and friend. For Elijah, burying his first pet is a solemn rite of passage. For me, it is another weekend chore.

We still have Mattie's ashes in a small aluminum container tucked into a little dresser upstairs. For some reason, we never buried them. I don't know why. It's hard to let go. Of a hamster, a dog, a parent, a way of thinking about one's self. Everything is always changing.

Elijah was six when we got Nibbles. In a few years he will go to college and Ruthie will follow a couple of years after that. The monsters that lived with us as babies are gone, replaced by lovely children who clear their dishes at night, sometimes without even being screamed at to do so. Soon they will be adults, and maybe one day, parents themselves. But right now they are still young and they want a cat. Everybody does, except for me. This Saturday we are getting a cat.

CHAPTER 19

i hope he's nice

I am twenty-seven years old, Martha is twenty-nine. In six months we will leave New York. In eighteen months our new puppy, Mattie, will be dead. Three years from now we will have a son, and two years after that a daughter. One day I will be writing these words and trying to remember what it was like to be twenty-seven and about to join my life with this girl that I love. If I could reach back to that day and tell myself anything, it would be this: "You guys are going to be okay." I could have used the advice because right now, when we are planning our wedding, she is being a huge pain in my ass.

Martha wants to be married in a Catholic church. I do not. I would prefer to be married in a more secular setting, one that has some personal meaning for me: a riverboat casino perhaps, or a Taco Bell. But Martha is unyielding, and in the spirit of pretending to compromise, I have agreed to attend this meeting.

Despite my misgivings about even being here, I like the priest right away because of his Australian accent and because his name is Edmund, a name as creaky and charming as the old oak furniture in his office. Father Edmund is

Martha's favorite priest at the church she sometimes attends on the next block down from our apartment building. He is a lanky guy, around fifty. He is also a Jesuit, a distinction I do not really understand other than I know it involves the mastery of kung fu.

Father Edmund begins the meeting by asking us some personal questions about ourselves. He does not seem put off by the fact that we are living in sin. Nor does he seem to care that I am Jewish. In fact, he asks if we would like to incorporate Jewish wedding traditions into our service. The only Jewish wedding tradition I know is the one where you stomp on a wineglass. Can we do that one? He says of course we can. What about jumping the broom, like black people do? He says he's not sure if that would be appropriate.

He asks if we will be raising our children Catholic. I tell him I have no plans to raise anybody Catholic, least of all my future offspring, but I don't mind if Martha wants to give them Catholic instruction as long as I can balance it with "Everything your mother tells you is lies." He responds that as long as the kids are exposed to the church, he feels that's all that can be asked.

Where is all the condemnation I was dreading/secretly hoping for? Where is all the righteous indignation I was expecting/totally psyched to see? Where are the lectures about fornication? The admonishments? At the very least, I expected him to swat me on the knuckles with a ruler the way I have so often seen portrayed in movies about Catholics. In fact, throughout our conversation Father Edmund is so reasonable and nonjudgmental that I am beginning to suspect that he might not be a priest at all, or if he *is* one, he appears to be terrible at it.

After you are married long enough, an inevitable question arises: "Which one of us will die first?" We have not discussed this question except as it relates to life insurance and the writing of wills. But because she was the one who insisted we get both life insurance and wills, I am confident that she thinks I will be the first to go.

Statistically speaking, she is probably right. Men have shorter life spans than women. Four and a half years shorter, on average. That is four and a half years for her to think to herself, *I won*.

There is also some (controversial) evidence that lefties like me die sooner than righties like Martha. The length of the differential varies from eight months to nine years, depending on which study you choose to believe. So that sucks. Then, when I factor in genetics, I'm really screwed.

Martha's family tends to be long-lived, particularly the women, who remain spry well into their eighties. Her grandmother just died at ninety-two out on the scrubby Montana frontier. After Martha's doctor tested her cholesterol recently, he told her she could eat nothing but bacon and eggs for the rest of her life and be fine. Her blood pressure is low. There is little cancer in her family. Plus, she goes to the gym, which has the double effect of making her healthier while simultaneously making me feel worse about myself. A negative self-image reduces life expectancy by seven and a half years.

My family's health history is not so rosy. Among lots of other ailments, we've got cancer up the wazoo. Literally, up the wazoo. Colorectal cancer is as common in my family as whining. As a consequence, I keep a careful eye on my poop. Anything out of the ordinary poop-wise yields an immediate call to the doctor. I have also begun getting weekly colonoscopies.

I am not going down like that. In fact, I am not going down. The one advantage I have going for me in my mortal battle with Martha is that I plan on living forever. This is no idle statement. Sometimes when I am not looking at pictures of Fat Kevin Federline online, I read articles about advances in gerontology and life extension therapy. Although I comprehend almost none of what I am reading, I am convinced that the work being done in these fields will provide enough breakthroughs within my lifetime to allow me to remain alive for at least a couple of hundred years. At that point, computer technology will have advanced enough to allow us to upload our consciousnesses into a vast, interconnected neural network, which will allow us to "live," essentially, indefinitely, or at least until somebody accidentally kicks the extension cord out of the wall.

So that's my plan. Maybe it sounds far-fetched, but once upon a time I bet the idea of stuffed-crust pizza seemed pretty far-fetched, too. A lot of people make the argument that they wouldn't want to live forever but I do because for an atheist like me, death is the least good option.

I am not an atheist by choice. Were it up to me, I would become a devout follower of whichever religion offered the best food and most holidays. The problem is, I lack whatever that thing is that allows people to believe in a supreme entity who cares every time a butterfly flaps its wings. Which is not to say I am without faith. I do have faith, just no place to deposit it. So I end up just kind of carrying my faith around like a pocketful of foreign coins.

As I mentioned, Martha is Catholic and an occasional churchgoer. She was raised in a fairly devout household and unlike so many other Catholics I know, retained her faith into adulthood. Her religion was a nonissue for us until Elijah was born, when she told me she wanted to have him baptized. I didn't really know what baptism was other than I was pretty sure it involved a carnival dunk tank. She explained to me that baptism is a ceremony that welcomes Christians into the church.

My initial reaction was, "But I don't want my kids in the church."

She wanted to know why.

"Because I'm not religious."

"So why did you have Elijah circumcised?"

"Tradition."

"This is tradition, too."

"Religious tradition."

"So is circumcision!"

"That's penis tradition. It's different."

We went back and forth like this for a few days while I tried to wrap my head around my feelings. Clearly, she was right. Circumcision is a religious tradition that I chose to uphold. I was obviously being hypocritical on this point, although I have always been okay with hypocrisy as long as the hypocrite is me.

The larger issue was that, by agreeing to have Elijah (and Ruthie when she arrived a couple years later) baptized, I was tacitly agreeing to have the kids raised Catholic, a decision I struggled with. My feeling was that the kids should not be coerced into any one religion. That if they felt the need for religion later in their lives, they could seek it out for themselves. Martha's argument was that the kids should have some spiritual foundation, a vessel in which to place their faith.

"Why?" I asked. "I don't."

"Exactly," she said.

Oh, I get it. Crippling existential angst is good enough for me but not my kids? In the end, I acquiesced because giving our children a religious education was more important to Martha than *not* giving it to them was to me. I'm not one of these strident atheists who think that religion is only a destructive force. I do believe that a faith in God helps some people. I also believe we all need guidance, and that if some people get that guidance from religious teachings and texts, that's fine. Father Edmund, the priest who married us, said something that has since informed my entire viewpoint on religion. He said, "Religion should serve man, not the other way around," a statement so simple and obviously true that when he said it, I knew for sure that he was a terrible priest.

My favorite moment from Elijah's baptism came during

the ceremony when the priest asked each of us, "Do you re-
nounce Satan and all the spiritual forces of wickedness that
rebel against God?"

"I do," I said, but I had my fingers crossed behind my back
because I think a little wickedness is good.

The kids go to Sunday school now. Martha and I have
agreed that they will attend until they achieve their First
Communion. After that, we will allow them to decide for
themselves whether to continue. Personally, I don't think
they're getting a single thing out of it but I don't think it's
hurting anything, either. They have occasionally asked me
about my belief system.

"Do you believe Jesus was the son of God?" they ask.

"No."

"Do you believe in God?"

"No."

"Why not?"

"I just don't."

"What do you believe?"

"I believe in loving Mommy and you guys," I say, feeling
very proud of myself for that answer.

"What about Lily?"

"No, not Lily," I say, but I am joking.

"Dad!"

"Okay, Lily, too."

If I have any faith at all, I guess that's it. Faith in the small
love that keeps our family together. Faith in making dinner
and helping with homework and taking walks in the woods
sometimes as a family, even though I know the kids are going

to bitch about it. If I had to describe my faith in a single word I would say it is "earthly."

In the end, I don't really think I'm going to live forever. Not physically, and not as part of the Matrix. Chances are pretty good that I'll die before Martha, if not from butt cancer then something else. I'm fine with going first provided she spends the rest of her life in mourning. Black veil, the whole bit. On the off chance *she* is the first one to die, I will honor her memory by living the rest of my days the way she would want me to, in a succession of meaningless relationships with much younger women.

Like anybody, I wonder what death will be like. I used to lie awake at night trying to imagine nonexistence. It's impossible, of course. We cannot imagine the unimaginable. We can only surmise it will be "like" something else. "Like" being asleep. "Like" taking Ambien.

The only comfort I take from my lack of belief in God is the knowledge that I turn out to be wrong about so many things; hopefully I'm wrong about this, too. That would be great. I hope God is real. And if He is, I hope He's nice. And I hope there's an afterlife and I hope that it's at least as good as Saturday mornings in my house when Martha and me and the kids are all sitting around the table in our pajamas eating pancakes together.

What if when I was twenty-seven and sitting in Father Edmund's office, I had known how the next thirteen years were going to turn out? Would I have still done it, knowing what I know about the sleepless nights with babies and pointless screaming matches with my wife and all the stress and worry that comes with being an actual grown-up person? Would I have done it?

I have never regretted any of it. I mean, maybe my choice of words at times ("cunty" could have been expressed more elegantly, perhaps), but not my decision to go ahead with this life. I catch Martha looking in the mirror sometimes. I know what she's looking at. The creases in her cheek where the bedsheets have left their mark after a night of sleep, creases that no longer disappear upon waking. She sees the lines on her neck, the little lines around her eyes. She worries, as I do, about getting fat, about the veins on the backs of her hands. She worries, as I do, about becoming invisible. Sometimes when I try to take her picture, she will not let me. "I look terrible," she says.

The thing I want to tell her . . . the thing I want to tell you, Martha, is that you will never fade for me. In the beginning of this book, I mentioned getting older, how the word *forty* looks spindly and weird. Getting older scares me, too, but I would not trade it for getting younger. Time moves in peculiar ways. Fast and slow at the same time. When I look at you, I don't see whatever imperfections you see. Our faces are just geography. They tell us the story of who we are and who we used to be. I see you as I have always known you: I see you at twenty-five and thirty and now forty-two. I see you as a little girl camping with your brother and sister, a purple bandana tied around your head, looking so much like Ruthie does now. I love the story your face tells me because I love you.

That is the real gift of marriage, I think. When people talk about "growing old together," what they are really talking about is the desire to see somebody all the way through, to connect your life with somebody in such a deep way that the word *old* loses whatever scary power it might have had on us alone. Yes, we change. Of course we change. I am no longer the six-year-old on the Big Wheel, the nine-year-old receiving his first kiss, the fifteen-year-old getting his ass kicked in high school. Those are just stories I carry around like old seashells. Nobody cares about old seashells, but you put them in a big glass and once in a while maybe you run your fingers through them and feel their surfaces. We keep them safe and add to our collection, one by one, over the years, and maybe the kids take some of them along when they start their own families, and in the end, I think that's enough.

When Elijah was six months old I had him by myself in New York City for the afternoon. He'd been fussy all day, squirming in his carrier, whining, letting out little bleats of annoyance. Exhausted and hungry, I stopped at a Mexican restaurant to grab some lunch. The waitress seated me at a booth and got a booster seat for Elijah. There we were, two guys out on the town, sitting across from each other after a tough day. I remember his eyes focused on me, wide and curious. I gave him a tortilla chip to suck on. My food came and the two of us ate together, quiet.

When Ruthie was two, I was outside on the porch working. She was in her room, asleep. After an hour or so, I decided to check on her. I went into her room and her crib was empty. I stopped to think: *Did Martha come home without me knowing and take Ruthie somewhere? Is that possible? No, no it's not. How did my daughter just disappear?* I had a moment of movie kidnap panic, the kind where the phone is about to ring and a voice goes, "We've got your daughter." Good Lord, was I going to have to go vigilante on somebody's ass? Before I let that thought process go much further, I gave myself a second to work out where she would go if left to her own devices, and then I walked straight to the master bathroom, where Ruthie was sitting on our counter, her face covered in lipstick, the entire mirror coated in a thick sludge of Noxzema. Little handprints everywhere. We looked at each other and she started bawling.

Last night, Martha and I had a huge fight about which are the correct rules for Uno. She insisted that players continue to draw from the pile until they have a playable card; I said you only had to draw once per turn. "Are you telling me I have been playing Uno wrong for thirty years?" she yells at me. "Are you really going to tell me that?" The fight had been brewing all day: a hurricane knocked out our power and we'd spent the day arguing about my forgetting to fill the tub with water before the storm, her paranoia about every item in our refrigerator turning into Ebola, and our general crabbiness at having to deal with the kids during this inconvenience. Unlike in years past, this fight did not escalate into a referendum about our marriage. The words "I want a divorce" were not uttered, not even once. Like the hurricane, the fight blew over, and we ended up in bed together an hour later reading by candlelight. Suzy would be so proud.

So yes, I would do it again. I would do it, because as confused as I am about matters of the heart (and pretty much everything else), I do have my small earthly faith in this life I chose, this "déjà who" life I sometimes do not even recognize as my own.

Father Edmund tells us we are married and she has trouble lifting her veil so I help her and we kiss.

I don't know.

appendix

For those readers who wish to know the correct answer to the Uno question from the final chapter, "I Hope He's Nice," I have taken the trouble to reprint the relevant information from the Wikipedia entry from the "Official Rules" subset of "Uno (Card Game)."

> . . . If the player does not have a card to match the one on the DISCARD pile, *he/she must take a card from the DRAW pile.* If the card picked up can be played, the player is free to put it down in the same turn. Otherwise, play moves on to the next person in turn.

Notice that the OFFICIAL RULES say he/she must take "a" card, not "two" cards or "ten" cards. ONE. Hopefully this clears up any confusion readers of this book, or my wife, might have about Uno.

One of the things Suzy taught us is that keeping score is an unproductive way to keep a marriage strong. In this particular case, I was definitely right and she was definitely wrong, but that's not what's important. What's important is that we resolved the argument in a constructive manner.

Also important: I was right.

acknowledgments

Many people read early drafts of this book and gave thoughtful suggestions and advice. The thing they gave the most, however, was encouragement. Writing about myself in an honest way proved to be one of the most difficult things I have ever done. There were many, many days when I felt like abandoning this project. I am grateful for the people who kept me going when I did not think I could. Thank you Rob Burnett, Jon Beckerman, Tom Cavanagh, Kelly Oxford, Mike Birbiglia, Mike Berkowitz, Ira Glass, Kimberly Lorah-DiLestri, Jessi Klein, Justin Chanda, Jay Gassner, Ted Schachter, and Barry Goldblatt. Special thank-yous to everybody at Gallery: Alexandra Lewis, Abby Zidle, Kristin Dwyer, and especially Tricia Boczkowski, who continued to champion this book all the way through.

Thank you also to my family. My story is not their story, and I thank them all for allowing me to tell my story.